Guytar Publishing presents

Guy Lee's

How To Make A Living Teaching Guitar

(and other musical instruments)

ISBN # 0-9747795-1-2

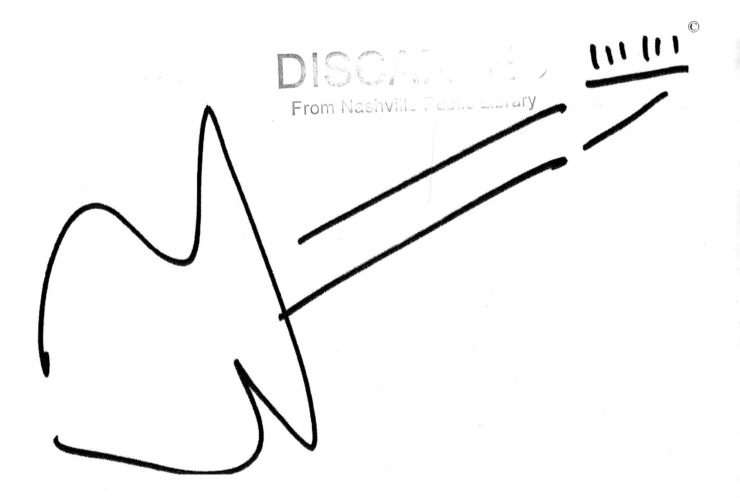

Thanks to: Epiphone guitars, GHS Strings, Digitech & RainSong guitars

Guytar Publishing
6765 Forks River Road
Hurricane Mills, TN 37078
www.guytar.com

copyright 2005 ©

Preface

This book is designed to be a business learning guide. Of course you can start to read it from the first page to the last page, but I wrote it so you could open up the book anywhere and learn something about successful teaching. My personal experience from reading 'How To' and marketing books is from looking in their *Contents* sections and finding the chapters that appeal to me instantly. I would eventually venture into the unknown territories (other chapters) to seek more knowledge. This is the case as in many business volumes. These books are not novels and are usually not intended to be read that way. To get the most out of any educational reading material, start at the beginning and work your way through it. I heartily agree with that. But if you already have a job or two and are trying to get ahead and still want to maintain your chops on *your* instrument, sometimes leaping around is your only choice because of your limited time factor. Eventually you will read it all anyway. I just wanted to make a guideline that has worked successfully for me and spread the word to you. I certainly could have used a book like this when I started teaching.

I hope that those of you who have toyed with the idea of teaching guitar (or any other musical instrument) will give this book a good read. It may help determine whether or not you have not only what it takes to teach, but put you in touch with the organizational skills that are required to do it. Of course being a good musician is a must but many other factors come into play as well. Responsibility, honesty, a good personality, patience, and personal self-motivation, can all help lead to a successful business. Even if you just want to teach part-time, this book will help you set up your teaching business with an established, proven structure, with plenty of proven facts that will help eliminate many costly errors. Teaching will also help your personal guitar playing improve by a 100-1000% depending on how many students you decide to take on. I am not exaggerating. You will experience extraordinary change if you decide to teach on a regular basis as I did. Many musical doors will open for you. If you have been a little musically burned-out for the last few years or so, you will probably experience a new surge in excitement in your guitar playing. Even if you decide to teach just one day a week, ten 30 minute lessons a day, for six months, you can't help but hear and feel the ease of flow in your playing. Even the way you speak will improve. Not just in music circles but in other real-life conversations. Teaching will make you think before you play and think even more before you speak.

When teaching professionally, you have to come up with new ideas everyday, all day long. This book is designed to help you with those ideas and plant the musical teaching seed needed for you to start creating teaching ideas for yourself.

Other benefits from teaching are the gigs that will come your way. Maybe many or just a few but your name will get out and people will want to hire you. Not just the honky-tonks but the more prestigious venues because you might be teaching one of these large business owner's or manager's relatives and they happen to like you. They will call you and hire your band and/or you as a solo artist or whatever musical echelon you let be known that you are qualified to perform for.

Teaching is fun. It requires quite a bit of musical skill. Many students will be demanding. Marge Simpson once said, " I can give piano lessons (for extra income). All I have to do is stay one lesson ahead of the kid". You will have to be alert and be prepared. This takes work and responsibility but the rewards are immense. Give teaching a try. If it works for you, then you will experience an enhancement of your lifestyle.

Introduction

Confucius say, "If you enjoy what you do, you'll never work another day in your life."

Having a guitar in my hands everyday is a joy. Sometimes, as we get a little older (in my case anyway) the dreams of hitting the *big time* start to fade and reality begins to creep into our lives. Car payments, mortgages, utilities, kids, all come into play. As much as we would like to perform on that big concert stage, make mega bucks and please thousands of cheering fans, our paths do not always lead us in that direction. Many musicians start to feel frustrated and unappreciated. They start asking themselves, "Are all these years that I have spent dedicated to learning my instrument, practicing, investing in gear and going without what so-called normal society has offered to others for my craft, was it in vain? I am actually playing the best that I ever have and no one is out there to hear me! I really thought that if I was good enough and worked hard enough, success would naturally come my way.

No one ever knows what path music is going to take him or her. It's kind of like improvisation, which is the most attractive ingredient of music to me. When improvising, if I end up on that *magical note* at the end, it seems to make the whole precarious journey worthwhile. That *magical note*, at this point in my life, is teaching.

Over the last several years I have been teaching full-time for a living. I started with four students and took it from there. I had no mentor or guidelines on how to teach. I could have used a book to give me insight and direction, and prepared me for any business ambushes, too. Then many other factors arose while I was teaching such as collecting money, keeping a systematic schedule and just how to stay organized throughout this newfound venture. Very soon after my first few lessons I realized that I needed several teaching and business tools to keep my teaching business on a smooth path. After a while, my schedule was filling up and I was adding more teaching days until it reached five days a week, averaging twelve individual lessons per day, usually without a break. At that point I started to plan group lessons because I was running out of time slots to fill. I was teaching until 9:00 PM every night. My first group lesson was not a big success and almost burnt me from ever doing them again but I then designed a simple plan of operation and the group lessons became a hit.

In my book, *Guy Lee's* **How To Make A Living Teaching Guitar**, I have put together an organized agenda to help you make money and keep the money rolling in. Of course, it is about more than just the money, like how you have to continue to generate capitol if you expect to survive. The guidelines and insight provided in this book will help you maintain a teaching business either as a full or part time endeavor. These are my experiences I have learned through many hours of teaching and dealing with the public. These are lessons I have learned through many hours of teaching and dealing with the public. In this book is the knowledge that I've gained.

Teaching guitar and other instrumentation will keep your chops up as a player and keep you challenged musically on a daily basis. Being a music instructor can provide a respectable income for those who strive to make a living by remaining in the music field. Even teaching part-time will supplement your income and keep your playing ability in top form.

You can do it if you make the effort. Enjoy yourself as you spread the joy of music.

Acknowledgements

I would like to thank my wife **Frankie** for all her support. Her co-editor job kept a clear vision for me for this book. Her determination for this book to be finalized and printed kept the focus clear when it was needed during the duration of writing "*How To Make A Living Teaching Guitar*". She's the best!

My wonderful daughter **Stefanie**, who went on the road with me when she was a baby and even during her teenage years. She was a real trouper and still is.

Thanks to my guitar playing big brother **Tom**, who handed me my first guitar and taught me a 'C' chord and then asked me a few days later why I couldn't play it very well. I realized at that point I needed to practice without ever being told to. I play guitar for the same reasons now as I did back in '69 when Tom put that guitar in my hands, for the pure joy of it. My **Mom** was a great honky tonk style pianist with an incredible ear for music and a swingin' sense of musical timing. My brother believed that we siblings had to have inherited some of her talent which prompted him to first take up the guitar.

My sister **Jeannette** has always been supportive of any venture in my life. She actually seemed more thrilled and excited when my first book, "*The Guy Lee Guitar Method*" came out in 2003 than I was! Her son and my nephew **Scooter**, has followed in the Lee footsteps of being a pro musician and has now added teaching to his Resume'.

My **Dad** is an independent businessman. Always has been. My self-motivation and honest business policies are definite results of his autonomous life. Although he's not a musician, he knew how to crank that big tube stereophonic Hi-Fi in the 70s when I was a teenager. His Chet Atkins and Ray Charles LPs helped round out my young listening ears.

My friends and colleagues at Mary's Music in Dickson, TN. **Mary Shafer** is paramount in the retail music biz. Being a former teacher she's always there with guidance and great advice for any music or teaching situation. **Kathy Hobbs**, who manages and keeps the business running smooth. **Wayne Parker**, always helpful with putting the student's guitars in playable shape and encouraging me to try out new gear. Piano teacher, **Susan Tune Miller**, who always helps me with any musical question that I'm in need of an answer for. The young and hip violin (fiddle) teacher, **Derek Pell**, who maintains an upbeat manner at all times. Percussionist teacher extraordinaire, **Mark Ellis**, whose knowledge and positive attitude keeps the teaching atmosphere great at all times. Oh yeah, did I mention that we all have a good time and laugh a lot?

All of my music students that I have taught and in return learned much from since the year 2000.

Digitech's **Paul Muniz**, a cool campadre in the music biz world. Paul supplied me with the amazing GNX4 pedal.

Jason Sanders at Epiphone for the extra cool Epiphone '56 Gold Top for the book's front cover. That guitar is killer!

Guitar String Maestro **Ben Cole** from GHS Strings for the superb sounding Sub Zero Guitar Boomers and GHS stool used in the book.

The amazing, out of this world crafted RainSong WS1000 from RainSong's **Ashvin Coomar** and **Jeanne Carr**. It sounds as good as it looks.

Indi Olienick for her patience, publishing and marketing ideas.

Ed Grochowski did a great job checking and doing the final edit my first book, *The Guy Lee Guitar Method* and helped me out again by tackling this book.

The updating of the website and all of the technical advice and follow through would have been impossible without the professional help of **Steve Tangalin**.

Thank you everyone!

Chapters

Getting Prepared

Organizing your teaching business from the outset is best way to be prepared. If your business happens to take off, you will have all or most of the tools you need to keep the rhythm flowing from student to student. This chapter will help you design your teaching business with the necessary components. The **Business Tools** and the **Teaching Tools** are in separate categories to keep your trade more organized.

Business Tools

Writing Apparatus

This is a business regardless of the size of your operation, so be prepared. All businesses keep records. To do so you must have and maintain certain tools. Writing implements of various types need to be within reach at all times during the lesson period. Assemble an arsenal of pens, pencils, erasers, highlighters, magic markers and a cup or more professional looking holder if you like, to keep these utensils in place. If you want to use a cup or mug, that's fine, but why not get one with a music note or an image of a guitar on it. I have both the Eric Clapton and George Harrison/Beatles cups. Students like seeing something they can relate to. This helps makes the environment enjoyable and cool. Of course the writing apparatus are not just for keeping records. The student/customer will need a pen to write the check and you will need one for writing a receipt (more on this later). When your phone rings, be in the habit of picking up a pen immediately because chances are you will have to make some type of notation.

Cell Phone

Even if the music store or your residence has a phone (land) line, get a cell phone. Having two different phone numbers is an asset. In my case, my home phone has a different area code than my cell phone and the music store's phone where I teach. Some people do not like spending any extra money to call the teacher to cancel or reschedule a music lesson. This is where the two area codes come in handy. Do not give them an excuse for not calling. Basically what you are doing is making communication easier for your students. This will save and make you money almost instantly. Voice mail is a must. Students will leave messages and, in my experience, the voice mail is the most reliable source. The phone will be one of your most valuable tools. Don't leave home without it!

Remember to keep your cell phone charged! Invest in an additional charger that will plug into your car's dashboard. This has helped me many times when I have forgotten to recharge it overnight.

Furniture

Yes, furniture. You need a small table to put your book on, writing utensils, a calculator, guitar picks, CDs and various other items. I have my table right beside me and use it constantly. I also highly recommend a good chair* for you to sit in. Your posture will be tested while sitting during long periods of teaching. You also need a chair for your student plus at least two extras. When friends and family come along, they like to watch the lesson and this leads to more students (more on this later). A footstool (more on this later, too) is recommended for the shorter students.

After you get settled in teaching, look for a chair that will give your back support. Hours and hours of teaching can take its toll your body. Leaning over, bending and moving the seat of your chair can be pushing the envelope with your back.

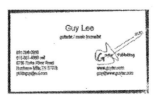

Business Cards

Keep it simple with the basic information. Underneath your name you may want put *Music Teacher* or *Guitar Instructor*, whatever title fits. Include your phone numbers, email and website address. A picture of a guitar or music notes adds a nice professional touch. This helps when people are searching through their wallet or purse for your phone number. The music symbols will grab their attention. If you teach at a store, you may want to add the store's name, address and phone numbers as well. If you teach at home you might want to put your address on the card. That would be your call. Having the town that I live in printed on my business card makes for good conversation and that leads to people feeling comfortable and becoming future students. When someone recognizes the town's name, they will often ask, "do you know so and so?" This will lead to a more comfortable conversation. It will put potential customers at ease. When I started out teaching I used to make the business cards on my computer but it got to a point where it was too time consuming to make them and believe me, time is money. So I went to printer and had 1000 cards made. The convenience of having a supply of business cards was immediate. Don't be shy. Hand those cards out to everyone, everyday. Professional cards look and feel better and leave a stronger impression than homemade ones.

Get a few of those plastic business cardholders for you to place your business cards on counter tops.

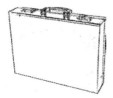

Briefcase

It doesn't have to be like The Blues Brothers but that would work well too. A briefcase will give you, the teacher, a higher status just for carrying one. It says that you are well organized and professional without saying a word. Also it gives you a place for your itinerary book, extra sheet music, pens, more business cards, pencils and so forth. A leather or aluminum briefcase or even a book bag would do just fine. You can find nice ones from about $20 and up. I actually use a briefcase size book satchel because it has a carrying strap that comes in handy when I am holding a guitar case with one hand. It frees the other hand for opening and closing doors. We all know how clumsy and awkward it can be getting a guitar case through a door. Just having the satchel over my shoulder enables me to maneuver more easily.

If you want to keep it locked, I suggest a briefcase with a combination lock, but if the one you like has a key lock, keep a spare key hidden in your teaching facilities for emergencies.

Receipt Book

Always give the payer a receipt, especially if cash is involved. A lot of payers don't care about a receipt if they have written you a check but give them one anyway. Buy a receipt book from any office supply or department store. Don't worry about having some special receipts made up at a printer. The store bought kind work just fine. Go with the larger receipt books for the advantage of more writing space. They provide a copy for you (which stays in the receipt book) and one for the payer. Write the receipt out to the payer's name. Most of the receipts have an area with word 'for' starting a blank line. I usually put in 'guitar lessons' or 'bass lessons' or even 'music lessons'. If the student is not the payer you can write in 'John Doe's guitar lessons'. This just keeps the paid/receipt exchange description clearer and a bit more precise. I also recommend including which month's lesson is being paid for. If they pay every few weeks, write each date separately e.g. 01-13-04, 01-20-04, 01-27-04 and so on. Always sign and date the receipt. Take the time to do this. This will protect you and the payer from any discrepancies. If you have a copier available you can copy the check and file it. The more records you keep, the better off you are. See page 45 for example.

Business Tools Check List

Here's a quick check-off list of items that you will need to manage you business with efficiency:

- ❑ Pens
- ❑ Pencils
- ❑ Highlighters
- ❑ Scissors
- ❑ Notepad
- ❑ Cell Phone
- ❑ Chairs
- ❑ Small Table
- ❑ Business Cards
- ❑ Briefcase
- ❑ Itinerary Book

- ❑ Stapler
- ❑ Paperclips
- ❑ Post It Notes
- ❑ Eraser
- ❑ Storage Tray
- ❑ Door Stop
- ❑ Push Pins/Thumbtacks
- ❑ Black Magic Marker
- ❑ Calendar
- ❑ Scotch Tape
- ❑ Rubberbands

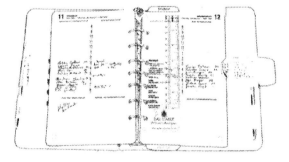

Itinerary

An appointment book is definite requirement. This appointment book must be in your possession before you start your teaching business. If you write a student's name and phone number on piece of paper it will probably disappear. Go to an office supply or a department store and find an appointment book that works for you. *Do not use a legal pad or a little pocket notebook.* Remember, this is a business and it must look and operate like one! The teacher has to keep records of the student's lesson time and payment schedule in a legible and organized manner. When choosing a book, make sure it has an area to write in names at thirty minute increments and will go up to at least 9:00 PM. Writing in pencil makes a lot of sense because of schedule changes. I personally write in pen because I can see it better. I use a whiteout pen or little white adhesive strips to cover my changes. After trying a few different books, I finally settled on a Daytimer®. They sent me a great looking book with my name engraved on the cover. This makes a big impression when talking with potential students about lessons. If they have never met you before and they notice the appearance of this professional itinerary book with your name on it, the first impression that they get is one of a qualified teacher, you.

Check out the photo on the book's cover of the appointment book sitting on the guitar amplifier.

Teaching Tools

Software

Invest in some music printing software. There are several brands such as MusEdit, G7, Cakewalk and others. Many music software companies will have sample downloads for you to familiarize yourself with. Discover what works best for you and your PC or Mac. Printing out music notes, TAB and chord blocks will make the music easy to read and maintain a professional appearance.

Music Stand

One of those heavy black music stands works best. I have tried the lightweight wire stands and they have trouble holding and keeping the music book's pages open, although they work well for single sheets of music. The heavy black stands (like the ones seen in school band rooms) will save you time and aggravation during your teaching session. Keep some clothespins or chip bag clips nearby to keep the thick music books open. The spiral bound music books are a breeze to work with. For one-on-one lessons I recommend using just one stand for you and your student to work off of. This will help clarify any subject matter in question because, well, you are both on the same page, literally. Strongly suggest that the student gets a stand to practice with. Leaning your head over a bed, chair or table is no way to practice. Some music supply companies have special lamps just for music stands. These come in handy at some point.

Power Strips

Always have one power strip or multiple outlet box. This is a must and two is even better. Having the built in circuit breaker (surge protector) is always a needed feature for protection against power surges, electrical storms or any other type of power problem. I am not an electrician so I use these phrases loosely. Read the package's instructions and the warnings that come with the power strip/multiple outlet box and consult a licensed electrician for any questions about their usage. Multiple outlets are of course one of the main purposes for these power strips. A six-foot, heavy-duty extension cord will come in handy too. Do not waste your money on those three-in-one plug-in outlets. They look bad and unprofessional. In my teaching studio I have four amps (guitars, bass & drum machine) and several effects and I keep them all plugged in with extra outlets to spare. If a student brings in his or her own amplifier or effects pedal, you don't want to be scrounging around unplugging your organized set up so you can accommodate extra musical gear.

Guitar Stands

However many instruments you teach, a stand is needed for each one. In my teaching studio I have several guitars, a bass, banjo and mandolin. The guitar stand makes you, the teacher, look organized and professional by having all these instruments on display. Instrument wall mounts* work well and look very good too. Having an extra stand for the student would be nice but is not totally necessary because they should have the instrument in their hands for the lesson. Guitar stands are a small but important investment. Some companies make multiple stands for three, five and seven instruments. Check into it and find what works right for your available teaching space. Guitar stands also save valuable time because every instrument is available for immediate use.

*__Note:__ *Always place the instrument wall mounts on the inside walls of your teaching studio. This way the hanging instrument will not be affected by the weather outside.*

Copier/Printer

The copier/printer has many uses. For instance, when the teacher writes out a riff or a musical phrase in tablature or music notes during the student's teaching session, a copy can be made for safekeeping or put in the teacher's file for other students. This gives students a significant practice agenda and a reminder of what they have just learned. Never take for granted that they will absorb everything that they are taught during the teaching timeframe of that particular lesson day. Also, a lot of students like to take something tangible home from their first couple of lessons to feel like that they have something material to show for their lessons. This helps them feel like they are getting their money's worth. Write with black ink for the best results when making a copy.

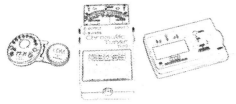

Tuners/Effects/Pedals

Always have an electronic chromatic tuner. Several of these new bands, even Hendrix in many cases, tuned down a half step or semitone and some even more. If you wish to teach some of these songs via a CD, instruments will have to be retuned. Many of the new multi effects pedals have tuners built in. As a teacher I use a multi effects pedal at all times. When the pedal is off, the tuner is on and I constantly check my tuning. The multi effects pedals can keep the teacher connected to instant distortion, clean twang, chorus, or acoustic simulation at the stomp of the foot. Because of the assortment of music styles I teach, it is good to have that instantaneous tone at my feet to give a tone relevant to the song being taught. Individual pedals are enjoyable and will keep the student's curiosity about guitar tone on the rise. Most standalone tuners contain a microphone for acoustic instruments and a ¼ jack for electric instruments. Pitch pipes are yesterday's news. Most students haven't developed an ear for tuning at the early stages of lessons and the pitch pipe can be unsanitary. Electronic tuners rule!

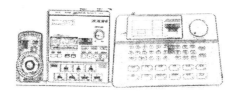

Drum Machine/Metronome

Timing. You have got to have timing. Without it music cannot be made. Of course the time proven metronome has been the most important tool of any good teacher for centuries. But since this is the 21st century, the drum machine might rule the roost with guitar students. First of all they are fun. The students will enjoy the sound and the variety of its technology. Strumming with a 4/4 rock beat from a drum machine can be a lot more satisfying then the click, click, click conjured up from the centuries old design of the metronome. There are newer digital metronomes that work great but they still have that repetitious clicking tone. The balance is that the students can purchase a metronome for a lot less money that a drum machine, but they need something with a beat counting value if they want to get to the next level musically.

White/Chalk Board

In the days of old, chalk was popular. Today, it seems that the magic marker/felt pen on a blank, white eraser board is the route to go. You will do a lot of writing and this will not only save the trees (paper usage), it will keep your teaching nice and tidy. What will you write? Music notes, TAB, words, band's names, guitar descriptions, pickups, etc...Many, many times you will use this *board* to help the student understand the many aspects of learning music. Get a stand or put it on your wall. If you have a chalkboard available to you it will work just as well.

Guitars, Guitars, Guitars!!!

Do not teach with your favorite instrument, especially if it's an expensive, or better yet, a prized vintage model. Unfortunately, your guitar is always in peril of getting nicked or scratched. Find a medium priced, good instrument that is versatile enough to use for the wide range of material you will be teaching. I have several guitars that I switch out about every six weeks or so. This keeps me from getting bored or burnt out using the same instrument over and over. More on this later.

Enlighten the student about the many different kinds of guitars & styles, For instance:

- Solid Bodied Guitar
- Semi-Hollow Bodied Guitar
- Slide Guitar
- Classical Guitar
- Resonator Guitar
- Banjo Guitar

- Bass Guitar
- Baritone Guitar
- 12-String Guitar
- 9-String Guitar
- Archtop Guitar
- Steel String Acoustic Guitar

Sometimes new students will want to learn how play a guitar from watching someone on TV or someone they have seen in a concert setting but they're not really sure exactly what kind of guitar that artist was playing. You can help solve this puzzle and put in the student's hand the musical instrument they really wanted to play in the first place. Now if they have already bought, say a classical/nylon string guitar and want to play blues, tell them what they have is fine for starting out but if they continue with the lessons they should get a guitar more suited for that genre of music.

Electric Guitars – Single coils, P90s and humbucking pickups, inform your students of their values and sounds. Maple, ebony, and rosewood fretboards that are standard on electric guitars, explain the differences and their pros and cons. The maple is slicker but brighter tone-wise and easier to see on a darker stage. Ebony has a smooth feel but is hard and deep in tone as well as more expensive and rosewood has a meatier tone but the wood tends to dry out if not coated occasionally with lemon oil. These are just simple examples of differences between electric guitar necks. That is what the majority of your students need. Give them *simple* examples for their electric guitar education.

Acoustic Guitars – Solid tops (cedar, spruce, maple...), laminated tops, mahogany, rosewood or maple sides. Necks made from maple and mahogany. Talk the wood lingo with your students. If you are not sure what is what, do some research and have a short conversation with the students that want to know. By educating them you will educate yourself!

Students are usually curious about why one Strat® or Les Paul® is $500 to $1000 more than another one. Of course, the wood, the paint job, the pickups and where the instrument is manufactured all play into the retail price tag.

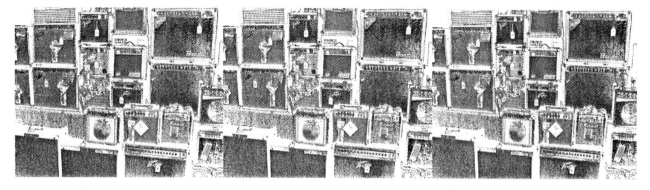

Amplifiers

I keep four different amplifiers in my teaching studio. Two are guitar amps, one is a bass amp and the fourth amp is for the drum machine. I recommend using small amps. You do not need large amps blasting away while you are trying to teach. With today's technology some of these small amps are plenty powerful enough. A large amp looming in your teaching studio will probably frighten away some potential students. Not everybody wants to be a rock star. Some students just want to learn to play their favorite song or pick the guitar for the joy of it. If the potential student sees a big amplifier sitting in the vicinity of your music stand, they might have a preconceived notion of your teaching methods and not join your curriculum. Even a P.A. (public address) head with a strong speaker would do the job and save space and money.

Many times novice students will not know how to operate their amp. They do not understand the process of dialing in distortion or for that matter, dialing it out. Tell them to bring in *their* amp and you will show them how to operate it.

The newer 'modeling' amplifiers that emulate all of the popular amps of yesteryear need to be addressed as well. Students buy these amps and have no idea how they work. They really don't know what they have. Help them utilize the amp. Educate them and yourself. Help them dial in a tone that inspires them to pick up their guitars.

Educating the students in the use of different amplifiers is a lot of fun for both them and you. They will see a huge Marshall stack and the smaller sized Fender Twin on a concert stage and not understand the difference. Most of the time they will not ask, so you just jump right in and inform the student why different guitarists use different amps. Explain why certain guitars match better with certain amplifiers. The mixing and matching of axes and amps has always been a form of creativity for the ears. Try to explain the never ending quest for the tone we hear in our heads.

Demonstrate the qualities of a *clean* sounding amp (the brand or model makes no difference at this point, just plug into the *clean* channel). Play a heavy metal rock riff through this *clean* channel to display how certain tones do not work well for every style of music. Ask the student why this doesn't sound acceptable. Then turn on the *distortion* channel and play the same riff. A simple demonstration like this will help students understand the amplifier's full potential and how the correct amp settings will provide an inspiring practicing tone for his or her guitar. Of course you will have to reverse this process so the students will fully understand how the *clean/distortion* settings work.

List the amplifier choices that a student may need. Help your students understand the sound and tonal differences. Let them know what will work best for their learning ability. For instance:

- **Solid State**
- **Tube**
- **Hybrid:**
     Tube preamp/Solid State power amps
     Solid State preamp/Tube power amps
- **Portable AC/DC powered amps**
- **Pedal preamps used for plugs-ins or heard through headphones**
- **Modeling multi-effects processors**

Guitar Picks

At all times have a variety of guitar picks of different shapes and sizes in your teaching studio. There are many kinds of picks for your students to experiment with such as pear shape, triangle, metal, plastic, fake tortoiseshell, small jazz picks and countless others. Keep them in a cereal bowl or a pick pouch if you like. I keep mine in a tin on a table beside me when I teach. This will benefit you and the students, who will, at times, forget their picks. Have some picks made up with your name and email address, name and website, or your name and phone number. Give these picks away as a promotional item.

Strings

Guitar strings will break. When you are helping to tune your student's old, funky strings, they can break. It is technically the student's fault because of the string's condition prior to breaking. Usually the students don't realize that their broken string is *their* responsibility. Explain the responsibility factor and keep spare strings for this situation because they do not yet know how to maintain their strings. Have an array of different strings because of the many kinds of guitar and string instruments. Electric guitar strings, acoustic (bronze, silk and steel...), classical (nylon), bass, mandolin, banjo and so forth. I am only talking spares. There's no need to be a string merchant! This small investment shouldn't hurt your wallet. Educate your students about the different gauges (sizes), so they will know about different size strings. For instance, rock and country music lean toward lighter strings, jazz cats and the heavy tuned-down metal rockers use heavier strings and so on... Explain to your students so they can choose gauges and select the size that fits their hands and musical styling. Suggest they keep experimenting to find what works best for them by investing $5.00 to $10.00 per set of strings until they know.

Guitar Cables

Cars get flat tires and guitar cables quit working, even the ones with that zillion year guarantee, so keep extras. Extra cables are always needed and used for connecting effects too. This way you won't have to unplug any cables to patch in a new pedal. Every time you unplug something you eventually have to plug it back in and that takes time and can be aggravating. Educate your students on the varieties of lengths, sizes, straight, coil, brass tip, angled or straight plugs, shielded, different colors (the light colored cables will get dirty!) unshielded and their unbelievable warranties (lifetime, ten-year...).

Blank Sheet Music/Tab and Writing Paper

Keep on hand many blank pages of sheet music. A large supply of manuscript paper is needed for a diversity of reasons. Writing music is one, writing chord changes on top of the music staff and even notating BPMs (beats per minute) for a reference point are others. Tab is required for picking out the riffs and for writing it out on your student's music homework. Just blank writing paper is needed for notes (terminology or music). I find that legal pads work great because they don't rip to pieces when being torn from the pad. Notebook paper can be a little hokey and reminds the younger students of school. You don't want that comparison to your teaching (the school-age students enjoy a different style of learning method than their daily public school agenda). Keep plenty of pens around. The almighty pen is great for writing checks when the student's lesson fee is due. Pencils, especially refillable pencils that don't have to be sharpened are great for writing out the music and/or Tab. Pencil sharpeners are needed for the basic pencil and always keep spare, standalone erasers around. They work much better because they don't smear as badly. See pages 63 and 64. Page 65 has a combination of both Tab and music notation lines/spaces.

The sheet music used for the graphics is from The Guy Lee Guitar Method.

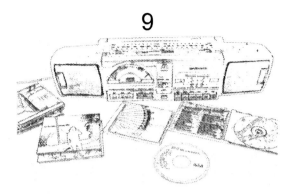

CD Player

This will be the most utilized tool in your toolbox next to your guitar (or whatever instrument you are teaching with). A portable CD system (a jambox) works just fine. The smaller headphone type that has an auxiliary outlet for an external speaker will probably be tedious to use on a steady basis because of the small buttons to push for its operation. Go for the larger jambox. There is no need to bring in an expensive system. Wear and tear is a big issue if you start teaching a lot of students on a regular basis. I realize that a quality stereo with higher fidelity would let you and your students hear all of the little nuances in each recording, but for the most part, the majority of students who bring in CDs to learn tunes are usually looking for the chords and the song's structure*. Of course, with the more musically demanding students (and this is a good thing!), being able to hear the more intricate parts of the recordings is important. The music recorded from the last ten years or so have so many tracks, it makes them a little harder to decipher because of the numerous layers of instruments. Earlier recordings such as The Beatles or Creedence Clearwater Revival recordings, you can hear every instrument clean and clear. You will personally benefit from listening and picking out songs.

Of course you, the teacher, will have samples of music on CD of what the student needs to hear for learning too. Cassettes are out. They are a product of the past. I refuse to teach anything from a cassette tape. Cassettes are too hard to work with and the speed of each tape machine varies and so does the pitch of the song recorded on the cassette. Students will ask you over and over again, "Can't you use the cassette this one time?" and I answer that if the song or riff is on a CD, I will gladly show it to them. Get a CD player that has the minutes and seconds written digitally for a quicker reference point when locating a specific part of the song that you are working on.

A CD player with a remote control and the readings of minutes and seconds is the route to go. It is much easier to pinpoint the song's solo, verse, chorus and bridge section by fastforwarding right to the precise spot. This not only saves time but a lot of aggravation too.

*You will have to chart these songs out. Write the chords out on a page with slashes for rhythmic strums. Use blank chord blocks to write out the chord's fingering and voicing. Use TAB for key turnaround riffs, intros and solos. Use a pencil. I know a pen looks and reads better but mistakes are common and it would eventually look like a big mess. Have your students help you write *their* song out. This is a great way of learning for them and stops you from being a song picking-out machine. *See page 66 for an example blank chart.*

CD Library

Keep a small CD library on hand with a concentrated effort on having an array of music. Keep at least twenty to thirty different kinds of recorded music available for the many varieties of lesson that you will be teaching. This assortment of music will be an ace in the hole in case no ideas seem to be available. The CD collections you see on TV are actually very good to study with because of the wide range of radio hits. These CDs are not for your entertainment but to teach with. I'm sure there's numerous radio songs that we would all love to forget or never liked in the first place, but these songs are for the student. Being a teacher, you never really know what everyone likes or is familiar with. These kind of CD collections are perfect for those lesson times when you can't seem to get anything happening. On some occasions, teaching a student a song that has brought some type of joy to their lives is just the thing to encourage that student to continue his or her studies with you. My teaching studio's CD library has saved many a music lesson from becoming uninteresting and dull. Pulling out a CD will bring freshness to your teaching for both you and the student, even if it is an old song.

Get a CD rack or holder. This keeps everything neat and organized. I have a CD rack that is a wire structure shaped like a guitar. This adds presence to your teaching studio and just looks like fun. Atmosphere, atmosphere, atmosphere!

Periodicals/Magazines

I subscribe to just about every guitar magazine out there. Take these articles to your teaching facility with you and share the information with your students. Most magazines are pretty varied musically regardless of who is on the cover. I explain to my students that when they see a magazine in a store and the band on the cover is one that they do not care for, it doesn't imply that the entire issue is not of importance ("Never judge a book by its cover!"). Actually, it is usually the opposite. I have found some great jazz riffs from issues with heavy metal headbangers on the front of a publication and vis-à-vis. Every guitar periodical has monthly lessons and is quite educational. This is a great source of new teaching ideas. On many a teaching occasion, I've used these lessons as the basis of instruction for my students. And you, the teacher, will learn so much more on your instrument. Since many of these publications have different levels of guitar instruction, all of your students can benefit from your research. I always suggest to students subscribing to at least one of these guitar magazines to keep their own interest up. Interviews with different players will always be of interest and a great source of information for you to discuss with students. The student enjoys talking with a teacher that has knowledge of their favorite player. You can talk with your student about what kind of gear their favorite musician uses and that musician's influences. A few minutes of each lesson can provide a musical history lesson that will keep the student excited about learning. Because of the popularity of different tunings, these magazines will keep you aware of who tunes to what pitch. The teacher doesn't have to be Mr. Hip but he/she needs to be aware of what is going on the music world today. Believe me, it will make you not only smarter, but a better and more knowledgeable player. Guitar magazines keep you current and that is important. Students will bring in a magazine with questions on how to play something. I respond by saying, "Great! Let's figure this out together." This makes them feel like they are part of the process. Along with the enjoyment factor, this helps students retain most of what you have just taught them. That is important. Learning music is not exactly the same as schoolwork because music comes from within.

Magazine Check List

- ❑ Lessons
- ❑ Interviews
- ❑ Gear Reviews
- ❑ Songs
- ❑ Advertisements
- ❑ Photos Of Musicians

I am a freelance music journalist and my work has been published in numerous music and guitar magazines. I can tell you that a lot of research and accuracy goes into every word and music note that is printed. I have to admit that I am really pleased with the quality of articles available in today's music market. Having access to so many music periodicals gives great opportunities to the teaching field. We currently live in a total information age so take advantage of it.

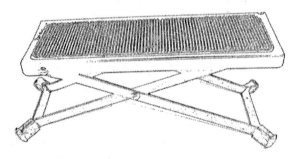

Foot Stool

As previously mentioned, this is one of the most invaluable tools that I have. The footstool has been designed for the classical guitarist but works great for teachers to provide a more comfortable environment for students. For instance, for the younger players whose feet cannot touch the floor from a standard chair, the footstool gives them a stable place for their foot (or feet) and in return, gives them more confidence in tackling their playing. Students who are overweight have trouble holding their guitar on their leg, so the footstool helps proportion their body so they can easily play their instrument. This is an overlooked but great tool for teachers. I use mine on a daily basis. This is an important teaching apparatus. Make sure that you have a footstool from your very first day teaching.

Books

We are living in an age of great learning and today's music books are immensely informative. Music books of yesteryear were frequently incorrect and caused a frustration for both teacher and student. I remember when I was just starting out on guitar in 1969, I bought the sheet music for The Beatles' song "Revolution" and it was in the incorrect key of F! That sheet music was odd to play for a beginner guitarist because of using a first position four note 'F' chord, a first position four note 'Bb" chord and 'C'! Nothing sounded correct and for good reason. It wasn't. That piece of sheet music was apparently written and transcribed with the beginner pianist in mind. It was almost certainly transcribed by pianist to make this piece of music simple, hence the key of F (one flat [b] note). That was the sheet music mindset back then. This was confusing and disappointing to a young learner. There was no way to play along with the recording under *those* circumstances. All that has changed now. Today's music books are generally accurate. They have the exact tunings, BPMs (beats per minute), correct chords and note voicing which are all presented with great clarity. Many books are written with the guitarist in mind. There is a lot to choose from out there. Continue to build your music library with books. This will help you stay on top of the teaching game.

There are more publications than just 'music notation' books that should be sought out. Many books are written on the history of music and there are countless biographies of renowned and unknown musicians available. Read about those who persuaded *you* to pick up your instrument. Spread the knowledge from the books you have read to your students. As long as you're not long winded, most will appreciate a condensed, narrative version of Django, Jaco, Jimi, Bird or anyone else you might have read about. Look at the world today. Many low-key music seekers use only the TV to obtain their musical background. It's sad but true. Help them out. Educate them about the excitement and perils of the precarious lives that our musical mentors have led. Help the student understand that to some, music isn't just about playing notes or trying to emulate a song verbatim, but about real lives and what many have sacrificed to be able to play music. This might sound romantic or even melodramatic but really, this is just the way great musicians have had to live their lives. Pass on this information. Most students will probably never choose to be a full-on musician but I know from years of teaching that they like to hear about it. Most will respect you for knowing how to play and teach your instrument and being acquainted with the history of your craft. This is a feather in your cap, I mean guitar case.

DVDs

If you have a TV and a DVD player at your disposal, use them. I have personally learned many riffs, licks and styling from this format. I only use selected parts to show students. They are not taking lessons from you to watch TV. Use a DVD segment to help explain how a certain phrase is played or to help you teach in a style that is not your forte'. Do not overuse this approach and it can be another stimulating tool in your teaching toolbox. Every guitar technique imaginable is available on DVD. Start building your collection and keep a library accessible for you and your students to watch. Stay 'in the know' and keep current with DVD releases. How? Read all the music magazines and/or get online to the DVD distributors and put your email address on their mailing lists. The current media groups are so approachable that you will have no trouble staying informed of what is new in the teaching world. Just do some research and follow up. Add the TV/DVD set-up to your teaching studio and branch out onto another avenue of teaching.

Facilities

You have to teach somewhere whether in your home, a music store, the students house, a small office or even a storefront. Each one has its own *Pros* and *Cons*. Balance the *Pros* and *Cons* for your own teaching facilities.

Your Home

Pros –

- No extra rent to pay keeping your overhead down tremendously. A tax advantages too. See your CPA.
- The convenience and comfort of never leaving home. All your gear stays at your residence in that perfect spot for *your* tone.
- No worries about *your* car problems, the student comes to you. And hey, no extra $$$ needed for fuel or oil for that beater of yours or that Mercedes you have in the driveway.
- Great access to your CD and even your record collection. Your music DVD collection could be of educational value too.
- People will know where you live for lessons. The word will spread.
- You are near *your* refrigerator. Stopping at the store is eliminated. Less out of pocket expenses.
- If you have pets, maybe they are the type that loves to be petted by anyone and everyone!
- Sometimes a change of environment from their comfortable surroundings will help the student learn more rapidly with less interruptions.

Cons-

- Students tracking in mud, grass or other unwanted debris.
- Maybe you don't want anybody in your home, especially strangers.
- Students will probably drop by unexpectedly for questions or just want to *jam.*
- Can't get them to leave.
- Insurance. What if someone gets hurt? Check with your insurance agent for any questions you may have.
- Maybe you don't feel like dusting and vacuuming today.
- If you have pets they might *not* like having guests in *their* home.
- Wear and tear on your floor. Plastic runners would be a good investment.

       Pro or Con- People will know where you live for music lessons. The word will spread.

Use common sense. Teach the lesson in your living room, den or dining room. If you have a bedroom that's a teaching studio it will work fine but don't have a bed in there. It is not a bedroom; it is your *teaching studio*. Have a professional name for your teaching surroundings (i.e. guitar room, teaching studio…). Leave the door open to your *teaching studio* at all times (it's a teaching room remember?)! Keep your house clean, especially the bathroom. You want return students. A good reputation is a must!

The Student's House

Pros –

- For the most part, you don't have to worry about having an absentee. This is where the student lives.
- If you arrive on schedule, no time will be wasted, even if student isn't quite ready. The clock in on when you walk in their door. Make sure that the student is aware of the start of their lesson time. For instance, when you walk in the door say, "It's 1:55, your lesson will start at 2:00".
- You can check out the student's music collection first hand. This will help in your approach to teaching the student more of their musical style and interest.
- Wear and tear on their place not yours.
- They can't say they have left their checkbook at home.
- Friends and/or family members around their house might lead to new students.
- Could be in a great neighborhood. Those signs on your vehicle will really pay if you are parked in the right driveway or in front of the right house.

Cons-

- Gas. It will cost you money to get there.
- Time. It will cost you time to get there too. Also, how far away is there home from yours? Is it worth the trip?
- Some people's homes are comfortable and some are not. It's a roll of the dice.
- Annoying siblings and there is nothing that you can say. It's not your castle.
- What if you spill a drink or knock something over? That can put the teacher in an awkward position.
- Try to use the restroom before you arrive. This will avoid any potential embarrassing plumbing problems, among other things.
- Could be in a bad neighborhood.
- Waiting on the student.
- Worst scenario, what if the student isn't home?

Figure out the student's house option out with pen, paper, and calculator to decide if it is feasible for you to drive over to his or her residence. You have to bring your guitar, amp and gig bag with all its goodies, load, unload and repeat just to complete the lesson. Don't be a slouch either. If the student's house it is, be prepared with your gear. Be the professional musician. You can work out a portable rig just for those traveling teaching appointments. Doing this might beat you up but if you only teach a handful of lessons each week it might be perfect for *your* chops and put some extra cash in your pocket. Using your instrument to pay your bills is still being a professional musician.

Small Office/Storefront

Chances are you will be renting a place instead of purchasing at this point. What your lease says about what you are and are not responsible for can be a big issue. Clarify with your landlord what you have to take care of; e.g. broken water pipes, broken window, bad wiring, and so forth. Have a lawyer check out your lease agreement and tell you in plain layman's terms what it means. Attorneys generally charge too much for this but it would be a wise investment for you. This should insult no one; it is just called 'doing good business'.

Do the simple math to find out if it is feasible for you to open your own teaching facility.

Figure how many students you propose to have and what you will charge. Then add up your proposed rent and estimated utilities. Of course these will be rough estimates except for the rent but it will give you, now the businessperson/teacher, a ballpark figure to work with. Nothing is written in stone. Learn to crunch the numbers!

Money taken in
- Money given out
= Profit or Loss

$$$

Any successful businessperson will tell you that keeping your overhead down is one of the key elements in turning a profit.

A **Pros** and **Cons** list designed for you to evaluate what would suit your business needs best. Use your *common sense*. If you spend more money on renting a nicer building in a high traffic area as opposed to lower rent in a substandard structure, then ask yourself:

1. Will my clientele number increase in the nicer area outweigh the lower rent?
2. Will I make more money in the long run?
3. Will a nice building help my reputation?
4. Can I even afford this rent?
5. Are there enough parking spaces available?

♫♫♫♫♫♫♫♫♫♫♫♫♫♫♫♫♫♫♫♫♫♫♫♫♫

Pros-

- Signs are your calling card and whatever signage you might hang or put out near the street should help bring business in your door.
- You have your own business address. A lot of people are comfortable knowing that your teaching is a business; in some people's minds it makes you more legitimate.
- Being a musician usually makes you creative and with your own spot you can live out your decorating fantasies. Paint your facility like Peter Max, bright and wild or just plain white. It's your football, you call the plays. I believe that music businesses should have a cool aura. Check your lease to see if it is okay to paint.
- Bands and group lessons can be taught as well as individual students.
- Make your own teaching schedule. You decide the hours of your own business. Many people work different shifts. It's been the new millennium for a few years now; so different time slots can be available depending upon when you, the teacher wants to work.
- Supplement income by selling picks, strings, tuners, music stands, blank music and tab paper. Don't make it a music store; just stock the products for the immediate needs of your students.
- Set your own working guidelines. More flexibility.
- If you have your own band, this will give you your own rehearsal hall.

Cons-

- The volume of your music playing could disturb the other tenants.
- Insurance is a must. Talk with your agent about the price. The only reason that this is in the **Cons** column is because it costs money and raises your overhead.
- Investing in cleaning apparatus. Glass cleaner, vacuum cleaner, trash cans and bags, toilet paper, broom, dust pan and other cleaner items. These items cost money right off the top and are needed as soon as you walk through your front door for business.
- Having the utilities turned on could possibly cost you a deposit or retainer up front.
- Supplying chairs, music stands, even carpet cost $$$.
- Phones and fax machines are a must. More money.
- Added responsibility of taking care of the property.
- In some cases, sweeping and cleaning your parking spaces.

Do the math before hand to avoid any financial surprises.

16
Leasing From A Music Store

All reasonably decent music stores should have some form of teaching facility for their customers. Many music stores provide teaching studios for teachers and are ready to welcome you. The music storeowners want you to teach in their store. They will make a good deal of money from your steady student traffic. Their sales will increase. Strings, straps, amps, guitars and so on will be sold just on your presence alone. The owner, who probably taught at some point in his or her life, is now busy serving the customers. This is where *you* come in. The storeowner can probably give you many teaching tips from their experience. Listen to them, gain their knowledge. This will eliminate many mistakes that might happen to you. Listening to words of experience can prevent mistakes.

Here are some *Pros* and *Cons*. Check them out and determine what will work best for you.

Pros-
- Great source of leads.
- Reasonable rent. Most stores charge a percentage of your daily take.
- A superb source for meeting future students in-between teaching established students.
- Convenient access to amps, guitars, strings and spare parts for both you and your student.
- People know the location. The store probably already has advertisement in the Yellow Pages and local newspapers. Most stores usually, automatically lists *Lessons* in these ads.
- The music store is a great meeting place and word will spread quickly about your teaching abilities.
- The vibe of a music store is just unbeatable.
- There is the possibility of you being hired for full or part-time work within the music store that you are teaching out of.
- Music store perks like promotional t-shirts, strings and other newly introduced accessories from music gear manufacturers.
- Possible commission on sales
- A prospect of attending NAMM (National Association of Music Merchants) shows.

Cons-
- You are at the music store's mercy for *your* hours of teaching availability.
- Working under other people's roofs can have an indifferent feel, depending on the folks who run the store.
- The teaching studio may be too small or even too big. It might just be ugly! You have to adjust to their settings.
- Even though you do not work directly for the store, the public associates you with that business. What you say and do reflects your position. Your own tardiness may cost you money but it can also give the store a bad reputation in the teaching department and that can cause problems.
- Limited time use of their phone lines. Keep the store proprietor happy and keep his phone lines open as much as possible.
- You have to pay rent.
- You are at the mercy of that music store's reputation. Good or bad.
- The music store might have multiple guitar instructors. This in-house competitive edge could hinder a number of students from signing up with you.
- Storeowner/proprietor not having any insight as to forwarding student leads to you.

♫♫

17
Tips For Working With Music Stores

✓ When working within the walls of a music store, consider giving the employees a hand if needed without putting them off. Between teaching lessons, if allowed, answer the phones when the store gets busy or help unload the UPS or FedEx trucks.

✓ Your product knowledge can make you an expert in your instrument field and could probably answer many questions of guitar buyers and possibly future students. The store employees will appreciate the help and will send potential students in your direction. Also the store's customers will see you being a trouper and spread the word.

✓ Most people like a worker; this will be good for your business standing. Before long, customers will start asking for you.

✓ If you teach outside the music stores in your area, go around to all the stores and offer your teaching services. Some music stores may not have the room to teach and would welcome a teacher. For instance, if a store sells a beginner guitar, the buyer will likely would want to know who they could take lessons from. It would be a feather in the music storeowner's cap to have a good and reliable teacher's name readily available. Leave flyers or business cards with all local music stores. People will pick them up. Never let your promo materials run out. Always keep plenty on hand.

✓ If the store is in a small chain you might be able to make arrangements to teach or even give seminars at the store's other locations.

✓ When the NAMM show approaches, check with the storeowner and see if you can get a pass. If you have never been, it is a grand event in the music business. New products and new ideas are introduced twice yearly, at the summer and winter shows. Don't miss it!

✓ When you advertise, inform the storeowner about their store name being in the paper or on the radio. Everyone likes free advertisement.

✓ If playing a jam session at a club or a lodge, tell the storeowner that you are going to wear one of their store T-shirts to the event. Another form of complimentary advertising for that music retailer.

✓ When teaching under someone else's roof, what you do represents that whole store. Be aware of this. If you are frequently late for your lessons, this reflects badly on the music store. Be conscientious. This shows respect for everybody that will be affected by your deeds, good or bad.

It is okay to teach in a different kind of storefront. It doesn't necessarily have to be a music store. I once started a music store in an upstairs room (approximately 30'X40') in my family's automotive paint and supply store/warehouse building. If you have a friend or family member who has a spare room in their arts and crafts store, carpet showroom or furniture warehouse, it is worth checking out. At the least, it will provide you a place to get started, and probably for little or no rent! But of course, for obvious reasons, a music store would be ideal. In other words, do not rule out any location. Procrastination will not make you any money in the teaching field.

♫♫

Booking Students

Advertising

Newspaper

I believe in advertising in the paper. It works, not quickly, but it works for me. The local newspaper seems to work well. You can run daily or weekend ads in the classified section for a reasonable sum. Check your local papers for prices. A lot of people read the paper. Even if they don't respond right away, I believe that the public likes toying with the idea of guitar lessons. A guitar lesson advertisement doesn't work like a sale ad. Many people consider the commitment of taking guitar lessons before making the call. It appears that even more people like to look at the local shopper's guide. They tend to sit on peoples counter tops for several days before being disposed of. My advertising in these types of papers seems to turn out good results but not overnight.

- The small 1" X 2" block ads work really well. Keep them simple. For Example: Advertising can help your business by getting your name out. You need to decide what kind of clientele you want and determine what advertising will attract them. Figure out your budget. Take your time, but do not procrastinate. Remember time is money. Always cut out your ad and put it in your teaching area. I usually take a push/pull pin and stick the ad up on my wall. Students will see it and start talking. Word of mouth from your newspaper ad can spread pretty quickly. Ask your new students where they learned about you.

- Using the small type want ad section can be economical. These kinds of ads can be run every week and not break your advertising budget. At this point you might be saying to yourself, "Advertising budget? I'm just a single, employee-owned, start-up business. I have no budget". Well, plan for one, even if it is only $5.00 to $20.00 a week. Anyone can afford that. I realize that some people may think advertising is a waste of money. It isn't. These ads can prevent you from having a roller coaster ride in student enrollment. If you plan to succeed, your appointment book must stay full. Even if you teach one or two days a week, keep those time slots full.

- Direct mailing to the masses can be expensive and most of it will probably get thrown away. This is just an educated guess (direct mailers make their living that way and design their campaigns accordingly) but from my own personal familiarity with marketing lessons, newspapers and weekly shoppers seem to get a hold of almost everyone in a cost-effective manner. Please don't overcomplicate the advertising approach, just keep it simple. You don't want a headache; you just want to add more students to your ever-growing roster.

- If you teach out of a music store, the store might want to share the advertising cost, be it newspapers, flyers, TV or radio. This will save you some advertising expense and still get your name out for the public.

Read the newspaper and check out the names of the journalists who write for *Local* section and give them a call. Maybe the newspaper will want to do an article on the new local teacher. It has happened for me several times... because I contacted them!

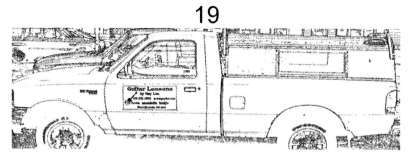

Vehicle Magnetic Signs

Your means of transportation can help fill your appointment book with new students. Welcome to the new millennium. Magnetic signs on the side of your car or truck are an inexpensive and fashionable way to advertise your business. When you work for yourself, you must promote yourself. This is not bragging, this is just letting the world know that you are in business for the long haul. The signs on my vehicle say this:

Guitar Lessons
By Guy Lee
615-555-1234   www.guytar.com
bass mandolin banjo
Mary's Music

I have gotten so much response from this means of advertising that I just leave the signs on at all times. Interested people call and also hit my website. I have even had people actually call me on my cell phone when they ride by me to ask about lessons. What? You don't want to be bothered? I certainly do. I teach guitar for my livelihood. Teaching is but a part of the business. Self-promotion is a full time profession and you need to be focused on that aspect of the business as much as your teaching.

Fast Food/Fast Leads When I pull through a drive through window at a fast food restaurant, the employee working the window sees the sign on the side of my truck and starts to write down the phone number. I hand the employee a business card and tell them give me a call and check out my website. I have had several employees gather around the drive-through window and talk to me about lessons. Many times the manager even joins in. This scenario happens quite frequently.

Here are a few simple tips for your advertisement on wheels:

- Always try to park where the signs can be read. For instance when your go to a theatre or a mall, park where the world can see your signs.
- Keep your vehicle clean on the inside and out. The curious might peak inside. Take you trash off the seats and floorboards.
- Be nice. Those days of racing someone to a parking space are over. Let the other driver take the space and be cool as you ride by them because they will read your sign.
- In this current age of road rage any obscene gestures will have to cease the moment those magnetic signs hit your doors.
- Have a custom front or back state license plate made up with your teaching information on it and attach it to your vehicle.
- If your state doesn't require a front license tag then have a custom-made front plate with your teaching info or logo.
- Have some *cool* bumper stickers made up. This way more people than just yourself can help promote your teaching of music lessons via the highways.

If you already practice these good driving habits then great, for the other 99% of us, ending these driving vices will only strengthen our personalities and will help add many more new students to our roll.

Having these signs on the side of my vehicle has made my awareness of being a courteous driver a full time activity. This will reflect on your teaching qualities and the results gained by all of this will be positive. Side benefit - you will get fewer tickets.

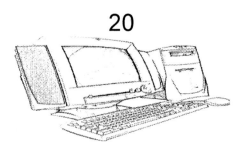

Internet

Get on it! Stay with the times if you want to stay in business. You have to have an email address. A website is even better. If you can't afford a multi-page website then get a single web page as your website. When I speak with potential students/customers on the phone, I tell them about my website. That way they can read about my qualifications and see what I look like. This seems to be an important facet of the teaching business. A well designed website screams professionalism! My website has a form that can be filled out and emailed to me. It looks specialized and gives an expert look. People don't mind paying for quality. The nicer the website the more chance you have of signing up more students. I also have two teaching videos along with two performance videos on my website. Links are cool too. Make everything professional with that positive touch. This way the student can check out your credibility and your chops. A web address looks fantastic in newspaper ads too. Remember, if you use the Internet, check your email everyday. Important emails about future students could be waiting. I have spent from $5 up to $800 for a website. There is some price you can afford regardless of your current income. Seek it out. Find what will work for you and your budget. There is always a monthly web-hosting fee. Just pay it and be a professional businessperson.

Brochures/Flyers

An inexpensive way of increasing your student enrollment numbers if you use your home computer. Whatever you might be promoting, whether it is group, individual or after Christmas lessons, the Brochure/Flyer approach is always a good one. This gives the potential students a tangible item to take home and study if they are interested in taking lessons from you. Samples are on pages 57 and 58.

T-shirts/Ball Caps

Get that apparel ball rollin'. Have some T-shirts made up with a picture of a guitar, phone numbers and your website address and of course, your business name. Let's just say that you don't really have a name for your business yet. Here are some examples that could work on a t-shirt or sweatshirt. Just insert your name. ***For example:***

1. Curly's Guitar Course

2. Guitar Lessons by Spike

3. The Six String Learning Machine

4. Frankie's Fun & Easy Guitar Classes

5. No Pain No Gain Stringed Instrument Seminar

People like wearing music oriented apparel. They always have. It's cool. This type of promotion goes a long way in advertising. I have been approached by many a potential student in stores, movie theatres and gas stations just because I was wearing a 'guitar' T-shirt. Be ready to hand out your business card.

There are so many T-shirt manufacturers out there today, the prices are low and you can have as few as a half dozen shirts or ball caps made if that is all you can afford. Maybe not all apparel dealers will work in low numbers but many will. Look in the phone book, check the Internet and ask around. Of course we all know, the larger the number of products that are purchased, the better the price. If you are working on a shoestring budget, you can figure in a dollar amount that will work for even a small number of apparel products. Oh yeah, don't give them away. $ell 'em!

Radio and TV Ads

Too much money. The audience would consist of many people out of your geographical area. You would then have to spend a lot of time responding to requests from people you may not be able to serve. But if you could appear on the local morning or noon time TV shows and perform, word would get out about your teaching. A lot of stations like to let local talent perform and usually allow the performers to talk about themselves. At that point you can tell the audience that you are a guitar teacher. Or as I mentioned earlier, if you share a partial ad with a music store audience it might be financially feasible to hit the airwaves.

Scheduling

Workload

Decide what days of the week you want to teach and the number of hours. This will give you a time frame within which to book your students. The students will adjust to your schedule if they want to take lessons. Some potential students complain about your available time slots because they have other projects that they are committed to. The ones who really want guitar lessons will adapt. Those are the students who pay on time and leave complaining to a minimum. Just a note*; sports activities have been my biggest competition, not other teachers.

I began teaching just during the weekdays but the law of supply and demand had me opening time slots on Saturday morning and then adding more into the afternoon. Saturday is now one of my busiest teaching days. For the last few years I have started Saturday mornings at 9:00 AM and booked myself until 3:30 or 4:00 PM. I book thirty-minute time slots with no breaks. Sounds crazy? Sure but there is a method to this time slot madness. When I book twelve to fourteen straight lessons, there is usually a cancellation or two and that is when I get my break. Maybe only a handful of times in the last few years have I batted a 1000 on Saturday attendance. Saturday is the day that most of the world has taken off. This is good because it makes students available for teaching, on the other hand, everyone wants to go out of town, go camping, attend a football game, hence the occasional unscheduled break…What would you do if you had Saturday off? There you go.

This is what I explain to some students: "I believe that sports are great for exercise. Exercising clears my head and helps makes my body feel energized. But when the younger students starts reaching the age of 21 or so and is living on their own in an apartment or dorm, they will be picking up a guitar and playing it, not kicking or throwing around a ball in their living room". As long as I can remember, sports coaches have not been thrilled with members of their sports team learning musical instruments. You will run into this a lot. Just be cool and never imply anything negative about sports. Many students do return to music lessons after their particular sports season has ended.

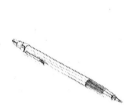 

Write It Down!

Every phone call you receive or contact you make, be sure that you have a pen or pencil in your hand and a notepad nearby. Enter the information just given to you into your appointment book immediately. If it is a *new student*:

- Student's name and/or parents name (if applicable) along with their home, work and cell phone numbers.
- Write in time and day and length of lesson.
- What instrument (e.g. guitar, bass, mandolin…).
- What they have paid $ or what they owe.

This will eliminate any double booking or confusion that may occur and provide documentation if there is any controversy. I can't stress good work habits enough.

Student Application Form

This form should contain contact information and the instrument the student desires to learn. A simple example is below. Do not overcomplicate this. It is not a credit application. The simpler, the better for both parties and I suggest keeping the paper size the standard 81/2 X 11 so they will store easily in a file cabinet or folder.

Student Application Form

Student's Name_____

Payer's Name_____

Address_____

_____

Email_____

Phone Numbers -
Home:_____Cell:_____Work:_____

Instrument_____

Private Lesson____   Group Lesson____

Questions_____
_____
_____
_____

Let the student or the payer fill the application out.

Student's Contract

♪ Some teacher's like to have an agreement for the payer to sign. These are not really binding (check with your lawyer to review any contract or agreement if you decide to use one). The theory is that some teachers feel the payer will feel obligated and this will keep the student coming back. Pretty much like signing up with a gym (most gym contracts are binding). I personally deem it unnecessary. I have toyed with this idea and have given it plenty of thought for my own teaching business. From my personal teaching experience, most people do not want to sign anything that they don't have to. I would feel uncomfortable asking people to sign a non-legal, useless document. Many will recognize this immediately and it might make you look like some type of flim-flam artist in their eyes. If they want to quit, contract or no contract, I would let them quit. You do not need the headache of a student who is *forced* to learn the guitar. I just want to state that this is only *my* opinion. Think about it and do what you feel will work for you.

♪ Now if your small teaching business turns into a teaching school I would definitely rethink my entire business plan and set it up accordingly. At this point, if you feel that some sort of a professional *contract* or *agreement* is needed, then going down that road would make sense.

♪ A completed contract is another source from your files that would contain the student's and the payer's personal information such as phone numbers, email and street addresses, and choice of instrument.

The Agreement Form

This is not a legally binding contract at all. Some teachers like to use these self-written documents. To some, they give security although a somewhat false sense of security. I personally do not use these agreements/contracts. I am providing a simple example because it gives the option of using or not using a signed form agreement. That will be your call. Many teachers like having them.

Agreement

Curly's Guitar Course

This agreement between Curly's Guitar Course/ Guy Lee and
_____(known from here out as the payer) will
assure on time payments due on the first _____ of every month in the
amount of $_____ for music lessons. The payer is responsible, even if
the student has missed his or hers predetermined time slotted music lesson.
For student's vacation time, Curly's Guitar Course must be notified by at least
two weeks in advanced or student will be charged. If a missed lesson is caused
by illness, Curly's Guitar Course will determine if the date in question will be
charged.

Agreed by:

_____
Payer   Date

_____
Representing Curly's Guitar Course   Date

Choose the day of the student's scheduled lesson as the payment due date for each month. For example, the first *Tuesday* of every month…

A **Contract** or an **Agreement** provides a hard-copy pact between the payer and the teacher, although this really depends on the way the contract is written and administered. A properly drafted and executed contract is legally binding to <u>both</u> parties but it must be handled correctly. Typically it is too expensive to enforce and generates bad publicity if you become known as someone who sues your customers.

Phone Advice

As I mentioned before, the phone will be your most useful tool and your main source of communication for booking students. You *must* develop a great phone manner. If you believe that you already have one, then you probably do. A lot of the phone magic is believing in yourself. This will reflect confidence and will lead to signing up numerous new students. Along with your self-confidence there are some guidelines you should follow:

1. Listen. Listen to what they want before you kick into your sales pitch*.
2. Be very polite, always say yes and no never use slang such as "yeah" or "huh".
3. Keep the conversation around three minutes if possible. Some salespeople talk the customer right out of the sale by not keeping their mouths shut. Yes, you are a salesperson at this point. Welcome to working for yourself.
4. Give them a short synopsis about yourself, i.e. that you have been teaching for two years, you went to Six String Music College, that you have performed with Johnny Rocker and Country Joe Bob… Just a little background to let the payer/student know a little about you.
5. I always ask if they have access to the Internet and give them my website address. This seems to be effective.
6. I mention that I am a father and have a child of my own if I am speaking with a parent calling for lessons for their child.
7. Keep a list (see page 25) of questions near your phone so you won't have any dead space when carrying on a conversation. You want to avoid saying anything dim-witted because there is some silence on the line.
8. Purchase one of those self-help speaking CDs so you can improve your public speaking. These really help. Check one of the larger book or CD stores or look online. These CDs have fine-tuned my phone and personal presentations. An articulate speaking voice is your key to booking students.
9. If a child or teenager calls, speak with them for a moment and then ask for a parent because children have no authority in monetary decision-making.
10. Always thank them for their call and tell them it was good talking with them. Be and remain positive throughout the entire dialogue.
11. Some will try and provoke you to talk about another local teacher. I always respond, " I am not familiar with their teaching" and move onto something else quickly.
12. When you get a message to call someone about a lesson, call immediately, even if you are in the middle of teaching a lesson, the student will have to understand and usually does. If no one answers when you return the call and you get a voice mail or a machine, talk to *it*! Always leave a message. People like that. They need to know that you are prompt and efficient. I have had many compliments as soon as I speak with a caller about my speedy return of their call. Keep your phone time to an absolute minimum.
13. Your phone skills will smooth out after a while but in the meantime you do not want to chance losing any potential students. Be prepared before you answer that first phone call.
14. Try 'practice phone calls' with your friends or family. It may sound silly but trust me it isn't. Preparing yourself and working on good phone manners will not only help you with your teaching business but it is a great character builder in the realm of self-improvement.

---

*Sales pitch? What?!?! Hey I am a musician! My music is first, man; I do not sell my teaching qualities or myself! Well welcome to the real world. If you want to work, you will. All working musicians have to sell themselves to bands, club owners and this is really no different.

Sample List of Phone Questions

Here is a sample list but you really need to design your own to suit your needs and style. These are in no particular order because this is a phone conversation and you want to be able to squeeze in a question here and there if the caller is a long-winded speaker. Sometimes you will do most of the talking. With phone conversations you will get people from all walks of life that want to know about lessons so you must be prepared.

1. How old is the student?
2. What instrument does he or she want to learn?
3. What is the best day of the week for you to attend lessons?
4. Are they a beginner?
5. When would you like to the lessons to start?
6. Which would suit you best, the afternoon or the evening?
7. Do you own an instrument?
8. What kind, an electric or an acoustic?
9. If I can fit you in today, would you like to come in and learn a song?
10. What kind of music does the student enjoy?

Demanding Students

Your time slots are your bread and butter. **Warning!** Some people will try to push you to your limit by canceling and rebooking their lesson time and will make your appointment book look like road map. I'm sure it isn't their personal agenda to throw off your scheduling but that is just the way some personalities operate. At first I always try to accommodate everyone. But common sense will soon alert you to those students who just don't care. Remind your students that they must be *committed* to learning an instrument. If they keep missing lessons apparently they are not ready, at this point in their life, to dedicate themselves to the arts.

Do not let the student run your business. Stand your ground and most will accommodate.

Demanding Teachers

Some teachers will frequently cancel the student's lesson time to benefit their own personal agenda. Of course, teachers are going to have to cancel from time to time because we are human. We can get sick or have a personal emergency that must be attended to. Some teachers abuse their self-employment circumstance by taking off to do their own thing at their student's time expense. Just stay focused about your scheduling. Remember, no students, no money. If you keep missing student's appointments, they will quit. We, as teachers, must train the students to be on time and that cannot be done if we do not show up ourselves. Your teaching reputation is on the line as well. If you are teaching in a music store, you have the ability to tarnish the store's reputation by not being dependable. This will cause unneeded friction. Sure we have to miss a day here and there, but the more that you are on your job; the better your business will progress. Just don't abuse your time off, and then when you do need to miss a day or take off early, people will understand.

When I cancel any lesson time, it is for a performance or gig. I let the student know in advance and reschedule their lesson time. Everyone is always supportive when I have to play somewhere because it is what many would like to achieve. The next week when I see the student, I always tell them what happened at the gig. They find it fascinating.

Make-up Lessons

The 'Make-up Lesson' question is quite the conversation piece among independent teachers. Teachers who rely upon student fees for their income are often put in an uncomfortable position when the question arises, "When can I make up my lesson?"

You have to begin by asking yourself:

1. Did they give me any prior notice before missing?
2. Were they sick?
3. Did they call five minutes before their lesson and leave me in a lurch?
4. Do they always seem to miss on their due date?
5. Are they a good student and just forgot?
6. How many times must I keep making the same student's lesson up?
7. Should I ask the student if they would like another time slot so they will be able to attend uninterrupted?
8. Was the student called into work unexpectantly?
9. Was there a family emergency?
10. Does the student even want to learn?

I can list countless scenarios questioning whether a lesson should be made up. Each case is different and should be treated as its own circumstance.

- Making up a missed lesson is your call. Many teachers do not make up lessons or they *say* they don't. Remember that the students are not just paying for music lessons; they are paying for that prearranged time slot. If they are not present, then you, the teacher, loses the time slot and time is money! If the student is sick or the weather is unbearable, I suggest that you do the right thing for the student and make it up. If they don't call, or are sick all the time or worse yet, sick when their lesson fee is due, have a talk with them and find out if they really want lessons because your time as a music teacher is valuable. Students can be trained to be on time and pay on time. Remember, you are the teacher, the one with the patience. At times I have made up lessons for those whom I refer to as 'Grade A Students' (always on time and pays perfectly) when they have just honestly forgotten or couldn't get away to make it to their guitar lesson. If they treat you courteously, return the favor. But be careful, at times, even the best meaning students will take advantage of your good nature.

- Another solution to making up missed lessons is to have one specific make up time each week. For example, every Saturday at 12:00 PM, a thirty-minute make up lesson will be available for those who want to participate. It will be a group lesson if fellow 'make-up students' care to attend. Even if all the students are on different level of musical ability this will still work out fine. Turn on a drum a machine and have all the students play a 'G' chord. Have the more advanced students take turns soloing, then change keys. Another positive effect will be that these students get to perform in an ensemble situation.

- Sometimes students feel that you owe them a lesson if they miss, even if they do not contact you. You must inform the student immediately that is not the way you run your business. You lost money with a dead time slot because of the student's non-communication. A minority of students will try taking advantage of you. Just think the scenario through before agreeing to make up their lesson in these circumstances.

Many teachers do not make up lessons; others do not have the time. Here are some scenarios and suggestions. Read through these ideas and do what you think is best for you and your student. Take every opportunity to protect yourself when dealing with a student about missing a lesson that you are charging them for. A 24-hour notice from the student is normal practice for a non-chargeable lesson.

Typical reasons for not attending the prearranged guitar lesson:

You will develop a rhythm after a while in dealing with students missing their lessons and informing you of it over the phone. You want to be nice because for one reason, if you are *short* with them, they will not want to call you if they have to miss again. Most people are not that comfortable with calling as it is. It will frustrate you at times but always remain pleasant. As previously mentioned (page 1), voice mail will let the students leave a message and they won't have to talk with the teacher directly.

- ✓ **Weather Conditions** - Of course, if the weather condition prohibits the student from coming in, then make it up or don't charge them and add the lesson at the end of their due period. Snow, ice, heavy rain, wind, too hot, or too cold could all be factors in a student's concern about his or her safety. If it is a reasonable concern, work with the student. In Tennessee where I live, it can snow three inches in one area and thirty miles away, not even a snowflake, so do not make a negative remark. Find out about the weather conditions in the other areas where your students travel from to reach your teaching studio. Today's TV news media have precise weather maps and radar systems that will give you a good idea of what is happening and where.

- ✓ **Illness** – When the students are sick, you don't want to catch it. When they call, thank them for letting you know and tell them that you hope they'll feel better. A few teachers I know require a 24-hour notice or they will charge the student. The student is actually paying for the time slot whether they show up or not. I mention this every now and again to reeducate my students to *my* rules of making up a missed lesson. What do you do when they call at the last minute? My experience is that you just have to wish them good health and when they return the following week, inform them that you need as much prior notice as possible. Without getting into any details, I let them know that I lost money because I wasn't given enough notice to fill their time slot. Every case is different. There are no set rules for this but you can tell when someone is taking advantage of you. Usually people are honest. Just work with them.

- ✓ **Had To Work** – Don't we all. Occasionally you will get a call from students saying that he or she has to work late and can't make it to their lesson. This seems to occur about 30 or 60 minutes before their appointment with you. What to do? Let it go the first time and be positive. Make a comment like, "I'm sure that you would rather be playing guitar". This makes the student comfortable. If anything comes up again they will be *at ease* when notifying you of any changes in their schedule. I usually don't charge them for this inconvenience. If this *continues*, I do charge them and tell them so in a very nice way. If they get upset and quit, then good riddance. You did the right thing by trying to be reasonable at first but this is how you make a living. Most people mean well, but there are always a few who want something for nothing.

- ✓ **Forgot** – I have never understood this excuse but it is used frequently. To try and avoid this happening at all, I tell the students (if they are minors) that it is their responsibility to remember when their lesson time is. Their parents are not the ones taking lessons, they are. I tell them this in front of the parents so everyone knows! Sometimes people do honestly forget, say for instance, they are shopping, a family member visits, or someone even falls asleep, and they miss their lesson. I am not justifying this, just preparing you for what you will hear. There is no universal answer of how to handle these 'I forgot' students. Take each case separately and treat them individually.

- ✓ **No Ride** – Transportation can be a problem at times for students who do not have a driver's license. Although this can be a common occurrence, it is not as frequent as the aforementioned excuses.

✓ **Vacations** – Yours and/or theirs.

- *Theirs:* Generally people will let you know in advance if they are going to Disney World or camping for a week in the state park. I usually take this opportunity to fill in those empty dates with walk-ins or make-up lessons. Make the most of it. You can't make any money with dead time. Don't be lazy. Utilize every moment that you are in the teaching studio.

- *Yours:* I inform all my students about two weeks ahead of my planned time of absence. Three weeks or a month notice is too far ahead and some students will not remember. Two weeks is good. I put a sign of my 'vacation notification' on the wall behind me. This way everyone who comes into my teaching studio will be able to read the poster behind me. Of course I verbally tell every one as well. Before my vacation, I try to squeeze all the students possible into *pre*-make up spots. I even come in to my teaching studio on my designated day off. This way I don't lose as much teaching income as if I were to take a vacation and leave two weeks blank. That's a lot of money not to make. Most students will want to work with you. They really don't want to miss their lesson so they will make it up before you take vacation time off.

✓ **No Shows** – The root of all evil in the teaching biz.

- Some honestly forget. If they have been students who have studied with you for a long time, use your best judgment in deciding whether to charge, or not charge them, for your inconvenience.

- If they don't care. Charge them. If they quit, big deal. Yes, you'll lose money but you are already losing money. You can't put a price on stressing yourself out concerning the 'not caring' students. You, the teacher, have to make a firm stand. The ratio of keeping students on your teaching roster in this type of scenario is about 50/50. Some students must be trained to call. Yes, we all just want to teach and have everyone show up on time and collect our money as planned but it just doesn't work that way. Get a rhythm going on how to deal with these uncomfortable situations and it will get smoother and easier.

Watching and waiting for the *no-show* students to arrive can be a negative experience and affect your day.

How you decide to make-up a missed lessons is one of the key ingredients of a successful teaching business. Basically, do what is right but do not let people take advantage of you. Once you develop a rhythm for dealing with those uncomfortable situations it will go smoothly and easily.

Student out/Student in

When a student quits, immediately write the word 'OPEN' beside that time slot in your daily planner to remind you that space is now available for rent. When I look in my appointment book and see the word 'OPEN' beside a time slot I know it is available. This works really well for me and guides the potential students to a more exact time slot option. You don't want your students all over the weekly map. You want it to be one after another. Get a rhythm going. This is good for business and keeps your time overhead down. It also makes for a good teaching environment. Students are coming in, others are leaving. The good word gets out about a busy teacher, you!

Do not plan your day with lesson time slots open. Do not start thinking," Well, after every four lessons I will take a break". This would be a poor business move on your part. Keep your daily schedule as full as possible. Do not practice bad work habits. You will have your breaks during certain times of the year. You need that full schedule to balance those economically slow times that you will experience.

Atmosphere

The tone of your teaching environment is an important factor in the budding sales of your available lesson time slots. Here are some pointers in ambiance: I have always invited interested customers to visit my teaching facility. This helps close the sale. Once people have seen where you teach, they start to imagine themselves being taught there. Some people naturally have a fear of the unknown. You can eliminate this by letting the unknown be known. The unknown being:

♦ What does his teaching room look like? Just taking the time to show potential students where you teach makes a big impression. My teaching studio is covered with photos of students I have taught or are currently teaching. This alone is an impressive statement about who you are and how successful you are as a teacher.

♦ You are making many unspoken statements by bringing them to your teaching studio. Your interest in their curiosity about teaching them makes them feel they are being treated with respect and they are being taken seriously about their interest in learning to play guitar. Once they experience a taste of 'what's to come' the prospective students seem relaxed and are ready to jump in and start playing guitar.

♦ When they are checking out your teaching facilities, demonstrate your instrumental prowess. I always play about 30 seconds of guitar for them while asking what kind of music they like. I then lean towards that genre in my playing. Play well for them. This is not showing off, it is presenting your capabilities to them. Make the guitar playing example fun.

Now the seed is planted for a new prospect to become a new student. Your teaching atmosphere subtly speaks volumes and has now been absorbed. These impressions are very important. I have added many new students and collected the cash or check within five minutes of introducing them to my teaching studio.

Atmosphere must be created. It cannot be bought. Some small currency outlay into your teaching area's furnishings to add appeal is always a good investment.

Bird Dog Fee

No thanks. We are not selling cars; we are offering an education in music, an enlightenment of the arts, if you will. Believe it or not, a few people have the audacity to say you *owe* them something for introducing a student or his family to you. They are usually thinking money or a few free lessons. This is the nature of some people. This doesn't happen often, but it will happen, so prepare yourself to inform these self-proclaimed 'bird doggers' that it is not your policy to compensate anyone for the opportunity to teach someone music. Funnily enough, in most cases, if confronted directly, the 'bird dogger' will nervously laugh about this if you handle it quickly and put an end to his or her entire 'bird dog' embarrassment.

Referrals

A goldmine. This is the best kind of lead. The prospect's friend or relative has already put out the 'good' word on your teaching abilities and they are ready to sign up. Always ask for referrals. You can be cool about it and not pushy. This should be a daily habit if you want to stay in business. I get some referrals from music store customers hearing and seeing me play. The word gets out and then the calls start coming in. On many occasions, music store customers ask me about lessons as soon as I stop playing. This provides me with the perfect opportunity to get more clients. If you are playing a gig, the same scenario will occur. Keep your business cards on you at all times. I check each day how many business cards I have in my wallet just as I check to see how much cash I have. I need the cards to put the cash in the wallet.

Store Sign-up Sheet

If you teach in a music store or any other business establishment for that matter, keep a sign-up sheet on their front counter. I display one of my brochures or flyers (for samples see pages 57 & 58) in one of those clear plastic picture frames next to the store's cash register. If they like, they can sign-up their name, number, email address, and the instrument they are interested in learning. Now you have another lead. Give them a call and book the lesson!

Business Cards Again?!

Keep your business cards on the same counter as well. Put them in those specially made business cardholders. This will keep them from sliding all over the counter tops. Check on your cards daily to make sure you have plenty in the holder and that they are not mixed up with any other business cards. People will grab a card and call you if they are uncomfortable about leaving their name on a public countertop.

Store Posters

Make up some posters on your computer and put them all over the store walls. While being in the storefront area, I have been asked many times about what I charge or what the length of the lessons are or what days I teach. I point to a poster that I have on the wall while explaining how to get signed up. This visual is helpful because people can see the guitars on the poster, with the money figure staring at them along with several other features. This makes it easier for anyone interested in taking lessons to understand the process.

Individual Lessons

How To Start

Welcoming

Greet the new student with a smile. Tell them *how happy you are* that they have decided to learn the guitar and/or further their guitar knowledge. If they brought someone with them, acknowledge the visitor's presence and invite them into the teaching studio. Inform new students where to unpack their guitar, especially if it is in a guitar case. Just to keep it simple and to avoid them bumping into other objects I usually have my students open their cases out in the hallway. The less confusion the better and it will make the student feel more comfortable because they are probably a little nervous about their first lesson. Point to the chair you want them to sit in and explain what the footstool is for. This will make the student feel relaxed. Then collect the lesson fee. More on that later.

Commitment

Instill in the new students the importance of being committed to their instrument. If they have purchased a guitar and amp and forked out money for a handful of lessons, they have a desire to learn. Teachers understand that learning to play an instrument is more than writing a check, but not all beginning students realize this. Take this opportunity to help new students understand what it will take to be a musician. Let them know that you will help them through this learning process, but *they* have to be committed and focused. This is important not only for them, but for you as well. If they understand the value of being committed you will have a better chance of keeping the student for a longer term and thus, a more profitable situation.

Fun But Focused

This is where your personality comes into play. This trait will keep your students coming back and word will spread that you are a friendly instructor who teaches with a high-quality standard. It will make the lesson enjoyable for all concerned. If students are having fun they will absorb most of what you are teaching them. This doesn't require you to be a comedian. Use your common sense. When you do talk about yourself, keep it short. I usually have a story connected with whatever particular piece of music that I am teaching. I keep a guitar in my hand for about 80% of the lesson, too. This way they feel that they are getting their money's worth and hey, how are you going to instruct them how to play without a guitar? I recently hung up a string of guitar patio lights in my teaching studio. People loved them! It was just enjoyable to look at. The guitar lights put smiles on everyone's faces and they look pretty cool too! **Guitars + Fun = Teaching Success!!!!!!**

The Student's Guitar

Most new students, and a large majority of semi-accomplished players, do not know how their guitars function, even when they have owned them for years. Point out the role of each feature on their instrument. The tuning keys, nut, bridge, saddle, string trees, strap button, guitar strap*, single coil pickup, humbucking pickup, pickup selector, input jack and so on. This will help the student with the 'guitar' lingo too. I start out by saying to the student, "even if you already know what all the components are on your guitar, I am still going to point out their names and purpose, just to clarify and answer any questions that you might have, because all guitars differ somewhat". Many students will ask you how you like their guitar or if it is any good? Be nice. Be positive. Even if it is some cheap six-string box, it might have belonged to their grandmother or their single Mom; the waitress who bought it with her tips, who knows? It could very well mean a lot to them, so avoid any type of insult or a slighting remark. Keep the lesson positive and upbeat and don't put your foot in your mouth. If the guitar is beautiful, then a kind remark should come natural.

I have students take the strap off of their guitar for the lesson. It just gets in the way.

Pedal Power

Keep a potpourri of guitar pedals around to spice up the lesson. This will introduce students to tone. They will learn the concept of creating different assortments of guitar sound images. Distortion*, chorus, delay, reverb, EQ, wah wah and countless other effects can be presented to an anxious learner of the guitar and kick in the fun factor too. Show them how to hook up these pedals by using a 9-volt battery or a 9-volt adapter and patch cables. Remember they have probably never seen these electronic devices before and they are paying you to provide them with knowledge of these discoveries. Many of the newer pedals have a built-in drum machine and tuner. Show them how they work. If you don't know how yourself, read the instructional booklet right in front of them and learn together. Many times, they will have an effects pedal of some sort and have no idea how to use it. Several people have never even plugged them in. They don't even know that they need two cables (sometimes students refer to these as wires, plugs or cords). This should be part of your teaching agenda. Teach them how to work with their pedals. This is enjoyable for all involved and everyone learns, therefore everyone's a winner.

Ohh!!!!! That nasty distortion. Many of the non-rocker students (and their parents) have a preconceived idea about distorted guitar tone. Explain early on that it is used for its sustaining abilities. The guitar cannot hold a note like a saxophone or a violin, but with the help of a distortion pedal, certain musicians can reach their musical intent.

Recording The Lesson

Yes, *you* can be a video and audio star! Some students will want to record their lesson. I think this is great. It will make you a little self-conscious at first and all that does is make you aware of your teaching form. You, the teacher, will become more comfortable after being under the bright lights once or twice. This will help provide the eager student with some worthwhile teaching information they can study repeatedly for the life of the tape.

Record Perfect Phenomenon

On the other end of the spectrum, some students can be exceedingly demanding musically. They want to be taught a song, but do not understand why it doesn't sound just like the CD when the teacher plays it or when they attempt to. Many do not identify with the art of record production and how diverse artists achieve *their* sound. Several of the people learning want 'instant results' and can't comprehend why this can't be achieved during their lesson. Yes, I know, you, the teacher, can sound almost identical to some famous players, we all can, but when teaching, the whole gamut of music is covered. Sometimes when we stretch our musical boundaries we find that we are a jack-of-all-trades but not necessarily the master of but a few. I attempt to educate students on the subject of this record perfect phenomenon. I put in plain words that the tone is in your fingers. As we all know, guitarists pretty much sound the same on any guitar. Impatient students will dwell on this. You can always find the TAB somewhere for whatever song they want to learn. Just have the student practice the TAB. Tell them once they have the notes down, you will help them with the phrasing. They have to do their homework first. Learning hard or lengthy riffs or complicated songs takes a lot of patience and commitment.

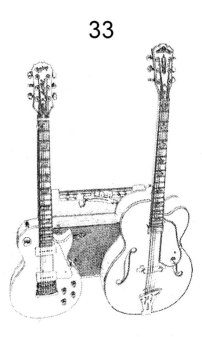

The Teacher's Rig

How to choose your instrument. I keep two guitars in my teaching studio at all times. One is a hollow body jazz box. This guitar is great for teaching students who use an acoustic guitar. Actually it is good for everything except those louder, distortion oriented rock tunes. Why use it? Besides being cool axes, they are comfortable and seem to help my personal sitting posture. Depending on how much you teach (I usually average at least 12 straight lessons a day), bending over to point to sheet music, string and finger location and guitar components all day can take a toll on my back. Talk to your physician or chiropractor for medical advice concerning your personal situation. Remember, I am just a guitarist. I keep a solid body electric around for the rock stuff or that twangy country grit. I change out guitars about every six weeks. This keeps it interesting for my students *and* me. I mean how many students have even seen a B-Bender, much less heard of one? You are not just teaching students how to play guitar but *about* the guitar as well. I let selected students play some of my guitars just to initiate them to a professional instrument. If you have a handful of different guitar models, switch them out every few weeks to keep your interests and the students up. The baritone guitar (if you have access to or own one) will intrigue students. This will be another new sound for them to explore.

Students will ask you about *your* guitars. When I bring a different instrument to teach with, they start inquiring about what guitars I play. It is always good for the students to ask questions about music gear. Bringing in a different guitar to teach with stirs up their curiosity and keeps expanding their interest in learning.

Challenge The Student

Give students a challenge musically. A piece of music that is difficult to play, but achieved by the student, can stimulate their need to broaden their listening and playing horizons. This approach would be something to tackle sporadically. Do not make learning the instrument *too* tough every week. Focus on all levels of playing. This keeps you and the new learner out of a musical rut. For instance, if they are rock students, have them learn "Fur Elise" by Beethoven or Chet Atkins' version of "The Wildwood Flower". If it's country they like then showing them the many chords of "Somewhere Over The Rainbow" or the opening riff of "Layla" by Derek and The Dominoes will let them rediscover their instrument with new eyes and ears. Classical players might have a little fun playing the power chords to Black Sabbath's "Iron Man". Introduce the students to a different genre of music occasionally and broaden their musical horizons. This makes teaching fun and educational. When learning is fun, the students will absorb what is taught.

Pet Peeves

Learning how to play an instrument is all about self-discipline and responsibility. All students must carry their own instruments, unpack it and tune it (or at least make an effort to) regardless of age. Some doting parents will try to help their kids through the whole music lesson process. Explain to them that for the children to learn to play music, they need to take care of their own instruments. Let this be known on the very first lesson. This needs to be nipped in the bud or it will get out of control. If you inform the parents at the beginning of the first lesson, then it should be no problem.

Listening To Music

Make this exercise a must for every lesson. Students who have listened to music most of their lives, as a rule, excel the fastest. Others that I have taught have learned the value of listening to music and have started their journey toward the thrill of enjoying music. I am not talking about preprogrammed radio music. Take this opportunity to share some of the songs that changed your life. If it had a strong impact on you it could also affect your students. Play all kinds of music, such as jazz, reggae, classical... Start to introduce your students to a new musical world. Awaken their musical spirit so they have musical choices. I tell the students, "don't let some faceless music programmer, who'll you will never meet, decide what kind of music and which songs you should listen to. These programmers don't have a clue about your likes and dislikes". Students trust and like you musically, so take this occasion to introduce a whole world of music to them. Naturally, some students will be impatient. There seems to be three categories of music listeners during the teaching lesson:

1. There are those who play video (visual) games. Typically, they just don't have the tolerance to enjoy something they can't see. Help them try to envision what music sounds like to them. Oh, some will laugh and you might too. But if they do laugh, just the idea might bring joy to the table. This might not be the result we want but as musicians, we are not used to instant results. The listening seed is now planted. Be patient and be a good self-listening example.
2. The majority will be passive. This is actually okay. Most can be overwhelmed by the prospect of discovering new worlds of music out there. Some just do not want to think about anything new to them. The guitar is just a hobby, a second interest of sorts. They just want to play some chords and learn couple of songs. At least they know what they want and can be easily satisfied. Their unspoken motto is to just 'keep it simple'.
3. Others will experience a musical awakening. These are the ones that might turn professional later or at the least, are dedicated while being taught.

Remember to treat all three categories equally. They are all paying you the same amount and deserve equivalent lessons regardless of talent or desire. Some will surprise you. Regardless of any financial commitment, you must do your best as a teacher to introduce them to new genres of music. When the students are being introduced to a new brand of music tell them that 'change is your friend, not your enemy'.

Explain the stereo headphone experience. Put on a Hendrix or a Pink Floyd CD and let the students familiarize themselves with the fun of stereo headphones. Even if they are not rock music fans, they can still enjoy this introduction to the new experience of traditional listening. Make listening fun for the student because without it, they have little chance of progressing musically.

The Tuner Again

If the guitar has a pickup, plug the tuner directly into it. This will stop any unwanted noise, which in return will allow for a more rapid tuning situation. If the student does not own a tuner, tell them that this is a 'must-have' tool and to bring one in by the next lesson. Teach them to use *their* tuners. Some of the features of similar brands are slightly different. You will simplify and explain this to them. If they have an acoustic guitar with no pickup, grab their guitar, put the tuner on your thigh positioned next to the sound hole and let them watch you tune. Explain the procedure that you are going through and that you will start teaching them how to tune on the next lesson. Don't let them carry on with small talk during this process. Tuning is essential. You can't play an out of tune guitar and it is frustrating for them to strum an out of tune 'D' chord not knowing why it sounds so bad. Being out of tune will discourage the student. I always tell the student that if their instrument goes out of tune before we have our next lesson, bring it by and I will tune it until they can master how to tune it themselves. You do not want your student having an out of tune instrument all week while waiting for their next lesson. You want them to be playing their instrument, training their ears to learn which note goes where. Being out of tune can discourage a student quick. Having trouble learning to tune is not a reflection on their talent. Some students have a naturally ability to tune right away. They might have been born with it or have grown up in a musical household. For others it will take time but they can be taught to tune.

Changing Strings

Spend a lesson teaching the art of changing strings. Show the student the entire process. I learned that letting them change the strings while I coach uses up an entire lesson, so I do it and explain each step. I make sure that they watch my every move. I tell them that I already know how to change strings and that I am doing this for *their* education. This is my course of action:

Help the students choose the correct gauge of strings that will work for their style of music and the kind of guitar they play.

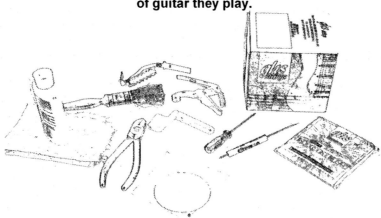

1. Make sure they watch how the strings are removed.
2. Dust and clean in the pickup or soundhole area.
3. Add a minimum amount of lemon oil to the fretboard if it is made of rosewood to prevent cracking and drying.
4. Demonstrate how to pull a string through *their* guitar bridge. This is a big deal. Acoustics have endpins, many Fender® style electrics have the string through the body, Gibson® style has the stop tailpiece or wrap around bridge and so on...
5. The art of wrapping the string around the tuning post to reduce slippage with cleanly stacked wraps. Cosmetically it looks neat as well.
6. Make sure the string is strung on the correct side of the tuning post. We do not want the student to learn how tune the guitar backwards by turning the tuning key in the wrong direction. Initial habits can be hard to break.
7. How to cut the strings. Sure it sounds simple to us, we have done it many times but they have never seen this process before.
8. Pulling on and stretching the new strings lightly to achieve more constant tuning control. This, of course, will keep the string's stretching time to a minimum.
9. Tuning the guitar as soon as the strings are put on it and not waiting because the strings need to stretch in tune to stay in tune. If the instrument is put away in it's case without being tuned properly, the strings will stretch out of tune and make the tuning process even more difficult.
10. Let them know that it is okay to make a mistake when learning how to restring a guitar because strings are relatively inexpensive to replace and we all had to learn. Everyone falls down once or twice while learning to ride a bike too.
11. Educate them about the tools*: string crank, wire cutters, screwdriver, polishing cloth...
12. Get in the habit of cleaning your instrument while changing the strings. Get that dust out!
13. Clean the fretboard. Next to the metal frets, use a toothpick or sharpened Popsicle stick to clean out the funk build up.
14. Use a small paintbrush to clean the dust out of the hard to get to areas such as the bridge and headstock.

Teaching students how to care for their instruments is something they will carry with them for the rest of their lives.

*See page 50 for Guitar Care.

Student's Excuses

They all have many reasons why they can't play a riff or chord. We teachers understand that it's usually because they haven't practiced. The number one excuse is, "my fingers hurt". I explain very quickly but in a humorous manner that "that's too bad". I jokingly tell everyone who uses this excuse that I'm considering putting a 'No Whining' sign on the wall. Joking, yet serious. They sometimes want to lick their fingertips. You have to remind them that licking will only soften their fingers and make the situation worse. Explain to them that the guitar strings are really filthy and they do not want to be putting their fingers in their mouth after playing the guitar. You will encounter these situations frequently. Other excuses are:

- "I didn't have time to practice this week". I tell them in an upbeat way that we can practice now.
- "My guitar is out of tune". The main reason that a student's guitar is out of tune is because they haven't made an effort to tune it. Some will bring their guitars in *way* out of tune because they did try to tune it! I let them know that they can call and come by and I will tune it until they get the knack of tuning it.
- "It's hard to the play this instrument". You're telling me!

I could go on and on but I'm sure you get the picture.

Elderly Students

Don't treat them like children. Elderly people are usually very smart and are just great fun to teach. They are also very motivated to learn. Some already know how to play and want to expand their knowledge. Many do not own CDs or a CD player, so some 'older' music homework must be done by the teacher unless he knows the music from the 40's and 50's. I was lucky. I played with a small orchestra that worked conventions and country clubs when I was around 19 years old. These experiences give me the background to pull out standards such as "Misty" and "Danny Boy".

Finalizing Today's Lesson

Allow a short time at the end of the lesson for the student to pack up his gear. The younger and older students will take longer to put their instrument in its bag or case and put their sheet music and/or CDs away. You sometimes get caught up in a lesson and their remaining time does not allow for packing up. Your teaching schedule will get off-kilter. Just make sure that the rest of that day's lessons adjourn on time so that the late lesson doesn't create a snowball effect. You will get better in this area as time marches on. You will soon learn which students need more time to pack up and make allowances during their lesson period. Some are just oblivious to these circumstances. You shouldn't hurry and grab the student's gear and put it out in the hall, but you may help them pack up in this scenario so you won't lose more time before beginning the next lesson.

Rewards

Some teachers maintain relationships with several musical instrument product manufacturers. These manufacturers recognize that today's younger music students could be tomorrow's big-ticket item purchasers or possible endorsees. These music teachers, myself included, work out receiving free promotional items that can benefit all involved. T-shirts, ball caps, stickers, pens, wrist sweat bands and other promotional items can be given to students who have worked hard to attain a musical goal set by the teacher. This is a simple, yet thoughtful reward/gesture on the teacher's part and will keep the student's spirits up. Another benefit is that the student will likely stay with your teaching program. Everybody's happy, the student (whose talent is recognized), the manufacturer (whose product is advertised) and the teacher (whose teaching schedule remains busy). It is a win, win, win situation for all involved. Rewarding students can be a very positive and upbeat action. Those who excel, desire to be acknowledged.

Group Lessons

Getting Them Together

Signing Them Up

Print up at least 100 brochures. On these brochures indicate the price, place, date, time and length of your group lessons. Mine are for eight-week intervals. This will be more than just a brochure; it will also include a registration form. I use a one sided, tri-fold brochure style for several reasons. They look professional and provide three sections for information (see example on the next page). I title the brochure **Group Guitar Lessons by Guy Lee** in the vertical position. The second flap (horizontal position) has all the must-know information such as the aforementioned price, time, place, age group, required book purchase, contact numbers and email/website address. The third flap (also horizontal position) is an application form for the student's name, address, phone numbers, email, age and a box to check for electric or acoustic guitar. The third flap is separated from the rest of the brochure with a perforated line for easy tear off. This way the student can keep the rest of the brochure as a reminder and a source of information after they have filled out and returned the registration form. I have a deadline date for the lesson fee on the brochure. This encourages the students to go ahead and pay upfront because you have a limited amount of seating available. From my experience, if they pay ahead of time they will show up. Try not to let them pay at the last minute if at all possible. This is a business. For my group lessons I prefer that the students are all beginners. I indicate this on the brochure. This way everyone starts on an even keel.

Chairs, Music Stands & Amplifiers

After you decide where you are going teach all of these students, determine how much room you have in square feet. I can fit nine students in my class teaching room and not one more. Ten just won't fit. This is not an airline so be careful not to overbook your class. This will cause terrible confusion and eat up valuable teaching time on the group lesson clock. Figure out exactly how much space you'll need. You do not have to be a mathematician to make an outline of your teaching area. To make your outline, fill the classroom with chairs, music stands and amplifiers. Take into consideration that playing a guitar requires more room because of its extended neck. Also, how many amps do you need? Ask the same question for guitar cables. Look at your student's application form and count how many are playing an electric guitar. There's your answer. You only need small amps. No bells and whistles such as effects pedals. A small P.A. head with one speaker would do an adequate job also. If the students want to use their own amp, that's fine as long as it is not a six-foot tall Goliath. Make sure there are enough power outlets for all the amps. Keep a power strip or two in reserve just in case. Now start to squeeze in the music stands, one for each student. Do not double up. Just because these students are sitting beside each other doesn't mean that they know each other. They all need their own space, even if that space is cramped. Those heavy-duty black music stands like we used to have in high school are the best. Of course, they cost the most. The lower priced wire type stands are sufficient and will do the job.

I would acquire a few packs of those "Hello I'm ..." name card stickers. Fill in the student's name legibly and have everyone wear them on the first lesson. Call on them by name while teaching the lesson. Speaking someone's name aloud helps me retain that name in my memory. This also makes the student feel a little more at ease. Saying, "Hey you!" or "Next" has limited appeal and gets old very quickly.

Stools are cool too because you won't bump your guitar into any backrests. If you want to get a little hip, many music manufacturers make stools with their logos on them and have them for sale.

How Do You Teach A Roomful Of Strangers?

Get everybody in tune. Immediately! You will have to teach them how to tune eventually but for right now get them all in tune. Be prepared and have a sheet of paper with a diagram of an 'E' chord on each music stand and explain how to read that foreign looking chord block map. The students know nothing at this point, so explain slowly and carefully about reading the chord diagram. One set of lines is the strings. These are the fat strings. These are the skinny strings. Don't call the first and sixth strings 'E's at this time. This will just confuse this room of borderline already overwhelmed students. This is completely new to them. Walk them through this process patiently. Put in plain words that the *other* lines are the frets. Then go on to clarify that each finger is numbered one through four. After everyone has a grip on the powerhouse 'E' chord, turn on the mighty drum machine and let him or her all strum away on the easiest 4/4 beat provide by that metronome of modern technology. Instant results! A roomful of new students will be wailing away on their own guitars. The fun factor is evident. These new students are satisfied and you will feel some relief and self-gratification until they are ready for the next chord or riff. It actually sounds wonderful, all of these guitars playing together. Like an armada of six strings!

Getting Around During A Group Lesson

Grab a long guitar cable; around 25 feet or so works best for teaching a group. You will need to be a bit more mobile because you will be going around from student to student, pointing out the correct fingerings and giving examples of what your are teaching. Having a long enough guitar cord will ease your movement in getting around the teaching studio. Forget a wireless system. Between the wireless system needing batteries and students wanting to know what it is and how it works, a wireless system would make part of your group's focus elsewhere instead of on learning the instrument. There is no need to overcomplicate a simple procedure like this.

Entertain 'em!

I try to provide a little bit of entertainment for my group lesson students. Why? Because we don't want it to seem like school. They can laugh out loud and have a good time. This is a pre-planned diversion from the hard focus of learning their instrument during that particular session. A few minutes away from any intensified learning will clear everyone's head. Even though you may be teaching in a simple manner, the student, when in a group situation, feels that he must come up to par with his fellow classmates. This creates some intense vibes that in return increase their drive to excel. Here are a few examples of my entertainment diversions and were off the top of my head. They just happened to work in the moment.

1. I had the entire class strumming an open 'G' chord with a drum machine pounding a demanding up-tempo 2/4-drum beat. All were listening to the sounds of the snare and bass drums boom pap, boom pap, boom pap… over and over. It had that bluegrass vibe about it. So I left the room for a minute and came back with a banjo (which is tuned to an open 'G' chord) and ripped into some simple bluegrass licks but with a little intensity and blurted out, "Yeee haaa!!!" The entire class was laughing and smiling and yet they never stopped playing!

2. I set a strong 4/4 rock beat on the mighty drum machine and had the full room of guitar players picking 'E' and 'E6th" on the two bass strings (E & A) back and forth, again and again. I then grabbed my white Strat®, added some major distortion and proceeded to start playing my six string rock contraption behind my head. They loved it and had a ball. Again they kept on playing. I informed all watching that the most important part of this procedure is to suck in your stomach! From bluegrass hillbillies to true rockers. Who would ever guess?

3. I brought in my B-Bender Telecaster®. This was like *show and tell*. No one in the classroom had ever seen a guitar like that before. When I pulled on the guitar strap with my shoulder and made that simulated steel guitar sound, they were just amazed. Then I went on to inform them that this is not a country-only device; just listen to Jimmy Page (Led Zeppelin) on "All Of My Love". That guitar demonstration opened the doors and minds of more than a few students starting out with what I refer to as "music genre tunnel vision". I preach to all of my students to listen to all kinds of music. Inform the students about the joy of learning new kinds of music styles. Tell them "change is your friend, not your enemy".

Recitals

After a few months of lessons, if you feel that the group is ready to perform for their friends and family you can set up a recital. This will give your students a musical goal to achieve, help their playing and keep their musical spirits up. No student needs to worry about their first gig because you, the teacher, will assure them that they will carry out the gig as a team. This takes any pressure off a would-be soloist. This also keeps the students re-upping the lesson fee until the recital is performed. Don't overcomplicate the recital. Keep to about three or four songs. Play along with the group too. This will help their confidence. Make it fun for everyone. You do have to be a decent master of ceremonies. That helps. The recital can be set at a banquet room, a lodge or a school. Find a place and be creative. You are a musician, you know?

Hit The Airwaves!

♪   **Radio Programs** - Another idea that worked for me is to get in touch with the local radio station (AM or FM). Many air local shows. Those are the shows that you want to get on. The DJ's are frequently musicians of some sort or they at least admire it. The radio programs are great to take your students on and will help you promote your teaching at the same time. It is a lot of fun. Students enjoy the radio gigs because they can't see their audience and that makes them feel at ease while performing. What a great first gig! This will be a memory they will never forget. It will have a tremendous impact on their lives. They will certainly tell their friends and family. This kind of environment will fuel their motivation and typically increase their drive to learn. The radio show experience is a great promotional tool and will get more students signing up for your lessons.

♪   **Television Shows** – Many local TV stations have their morning and/or noontime programs. You know the ones I am talking about. They have the local chef, quilt maker or other local talent being interviewed. These are cool shows. Especially since I believe highly in local promotion. Watch the credits on the programs that have the format that might work for your students to perform on. Write down the names of the producers and directors, then call or email the TV station. They will respond because this is what they do. In their minds if they have an ensemble on their TV show, then the ensemble's friends, families and schoolmates will tune in. This will increase the TV show's ratings. A recital like this can help everyone involved. Need I mention the publicity that you will receive for your teaching abilities? Thousands will watch it.

Check with the local cable access channels about their programs. Many cities have these neighborhood stations and they would be ideal for a showcase for your students. You are probably thinking "Wayne's World", but still, it would be a lot of excitement for everyone involved. It would be great exposure for your teaching business and definitely add to your credibility as a music instructor. The students will be happy, friends and family will be thrilled for them and this will increase your business.

Group's Conclusion

Many students will want to rejoin the group for another eight weeks. Others will want private lessons from you. Speak with each student and parent privately and determine what route they want to take after the group lessons come to an end. Don't wait till the last minute. Have the meeting around the sixth or seventh week. Give them some time to think things over. No one likes pressure. This should be plenty of time for the student to decide between a group or private lesson. After two eight-week sessions, I split the class into individual lessons. At this point some will be more advanced then others. It is now time for the students to be taught on their own. If you feel that one eight-week session is enough before splitting up the class for individual lessons, that is fine. Make the call on what works best in your circumstances. Of course a few will fall by the wayside but that's rock and roll.

Make Up Lessons For Groups

Missed group lessons can make a student fall behind and put a strain on the class. If the student really wants to learn and stay current with the curriculum of the group, you have to make an effort to help. Here are some suggestions:

- Make up the lesson during one of your vacant time slots at your convenience
- Have the student arrive early to the group lesson and have him/her practice an overview of the missed lesson
- Take ten minutes out of your day and give the student a quick lesson, touching upon all the important issues that were missed and tell them to practice even more then their routine so they will be able to catch up with the class.

You must be careful with this because everyone in the group now thinks that they are entitled to a free make up lesson. Remember; only make use of a time slot that is available, at your convenience.

Graduation Certificates

Let's face it. Everyone likes some type of recognition after achieving his or her goals. A certificate for attending your two eight-week music courses deserves just that. First you can see what your PC or Mac has to offer in the diploma department. Print a few different ones out to determine which one you like best. Custom design them with music notes, guitars or whatever represents the area that you are in. E.g. Waves if you live near the ocean, cactus if close to the desert, and mountaintops if next to a mountain range… Just try to be creative and make the certificate more memorable. Even check the Internet for ideas or just design one completely on your own and have them printed up by the local printer. The better the quality, the more professional you will appear. Find some gold seals and stick them on the certificates. Print them in the 8 X 10 dimension. Make sure that the student's name is written in big script. You, the teacher, use a fountain pen and sign it BIG! You do not want to spend a fortune. Decide on a budget, $10 or $25 for the lot. With a professional printer, the more you print, the cheaper the cost, especially if you are going to be in the teaching business for the long term.

Below is an example I designed on my computer in about thirty minutes. And there were at least 50 other examples for me to choose from. Be creative and make it fun. This example has *'two concurrent eight-week courses'*; of course you can put an eight-week course, six week or whatever your lesson time length is. Be sure to include the name, The Multistring Institute of Music Lessons is just a play on words and is fictional.

Certificate of Completion

This certifies that

_____

Musician

has completed two concurrent eight week courses from
The Multistring Institute of Music Lessons.

_____

Teacher - Date

Planning Group Lessons

If you are going to have an eight-week group, plan a certain lesson activity for each week. Here is an example for you to go by. This is not for the student to see. These are supposed to be your own personal notes.

Stay organized. It's okay to improvise. Use the *Plan* as your foundation. This way you won't look confused and disorganized. The students will benefit from the lesson much more if there is structure.

These are just *examples*. Be creative and devise your own guidelines. That would be more enjoyable and wouldn't have that scholarly characteristic. Have fun! Your personality will be your one of your strongest tools.

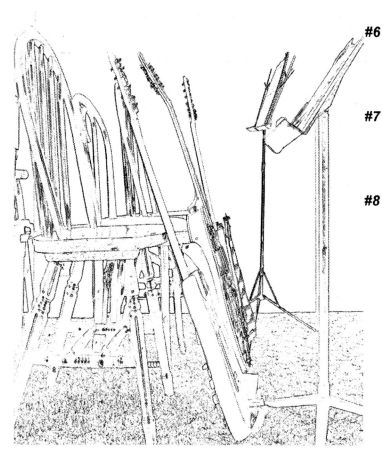

Lesson Week

 # 1
a) Explain tuning/getting in tune
b) Name and number strings
c) Teach 'A' and 'D' chords
d) Strum down strokes

 # 2
a) Two note rock and roll rhythms
b) E & E6
c) A & A6
d) D & D6

 # 3
a) Bring in drum machine
b) Practice up & down strumming
c) Split class – strumming and R&R rhythms

#4
a) Fun 'rock' riffs
b) "Satisfaction"
c) "Sweet Home Alabama"
d) "Rock and Roll"

#5
a) Recap all the chords learned
b) Use drum machine for this (a)
c) Four lead notes for improvisation

#6
a) Learn to read 3 notes
b) Explain 4/4 and ¾ time
c) Have class count timing aloud
d) "Folsom Prison Blues" riff

#7
a) Bring in different instruments
b) Swap instruments among students
c) Have everyone play in the key of 'G'
d) Use drum machine

#8
a) Remind everyone of last lesson
b) Sign up for individual lessons
c) Recap the most successful music played
d) Make the final lesson fun

Congratulate them all!

Hand out Certificates of Completion!!!!!!!!!!!!

Money

Keeping Records

Write everything down. All of it. Don't slack on this part. Keeping track of all your business dealings will keep you out of hot water. Honesty of course is the best and only way to run a business and you must be able to back up all transactions. Transactions mean: the exchange of money, lesson appointment time, changes in schedule, phone numbers, addresses, receipts and any matters that will cost or make you money.

Go to any office supply store or look online and find an appointment book that will work well for you. Make sure that you have enough physical space to write in names. For instance, when scheduling, I write in the student's name, amount of payment and I mark each week that the student is paid for. The last week before they are due I put an asterisk (*) as a reminder to tell the student that payment will be 'due' on their next lesson. Most people appreciate it and only a few act like you're a bill collector. The lesson fee is due and the payer needs to be reminded.

Design a simple form on your computer for the students to use to fill out their personal information. For example (see page 22), name, address, payer's name, as many phone numbers as you can get (home, cell, work, Aunt or Uncle's) and email address. This information will be logged into your scheduling book. If a student doesn't show, you need to give him/her a call. New students forget most frequently and they appreciate being reminded. On the form you may want to put in an area for referrals. This could generate other strong leads.

Some teachers use those pocket electronic 'I books' or 'handhelds'. If you are comfortable with these devices use whatever works for you, as long as it has the appearance of professionalism. The average person though, likes to see some things in plain old black and white.

How To Collect

Receiving money from another person can be easy or it can be uncomfortable. Make the situation as uncomplicated as possible for all concerned. Some people are real funny about money!

- Always ask for the fee at the beginning of the lesson. Don't be afraid. They are usually waiting to give it to you.
- Some will have the check ready and give it to you upon the start of the lesson.
- Others will have the check visual in their shirt pocket.
- Some do not know when they are *due* and ask.
- A few will ask if they are due (and they know they are!) to test you.
- Several will pull out cash without the correct change. If I don't have the change I will go get it on *their* time. Sometimes they will offer to bring the correct amount back after the lesson. This usually works out fine.
- Didn't know that they were *due*. They don't have the money on them. Most people will offer to bring it the following week. Tell them that you would like it today. They don't have to wait a week for their pay check do they?
- Keep the exchange of money clear and precise for everyone involved.
- Don't be defensive when there is a discrepancy about money. Stay calm and be cool. That is the best way to work out a solution.
- Always thank them when getting paid, whether they are good friends or new acquaintances.

What To Charge

I realize that if I put a dollar figure down on this page that it would make the lesson fee decision easy but life and business just doesn't work that way. And for many reasons. If I gave you today's dollar price for a guitar lesson, in a few years when someone picks up this book, that price would be outdated. Prices differ from area to area, city to city, and state to state. I go through a process to determine the bottom line of *what to charge*. There are several levels and degrees of figuring the cost for lessons. Start with the lesson's length and whether it is an individual or a group class.

- 30 minute private lessons
- 45 minute private lessons
- 1 hour private lessons
- 1 hour group lessons

Next, decide what would be the best way to collect the lesson fee.

- Weekly (per lesson)
- Bi-weekly
- Monthly
- Every 4 weeks*
- Every 3 months
- A 10-week group lesson
- Summer group

At this point I would call several music stores (5 to 10) to determine their rates. I even look all over the Internet to learn what teachers charge in different cities. This will give you a ballpark figure. My experience is if you don't charge enough for lessons, the public doesn't think that your quality is up to par. When I give a potential student my price and they comment that they can get lessons at a cheaper cost, I stand by my price. Never discount your worth. This is not the used car business. This is selling your hard-earned experience and musical knowledge.

$$$$$$$$$$$$$$$$$$$$$$$$$$$$$$$$$$$$$

Note: On collecting every four weeks, I ask that they pay on the fourth lesson. Most are willing. This will insure that they will show up the next week. If they are due the next week, sometimes they will skip and come in the following week and pay you, but not for the missed lesson. If you can collect on the fourth week, it will cover you and keep the student paid ahead.

My Story Of How I Charge

When I first started teaching, I charged students on a weekly basis because this was the protocol of the music store where I taught. I had no idea how this teaching *business* worked. Charging for lessons weekly was a disaster. First of all, I could hardly make any money. There was never enough $ to add up to a decent bank deposit. When people pay weekly or per lesson, they do not feel the need to come to their appointed lesson on a regular basis because they haven't made any financial obligations. The student's/payer's line of thinking was, "Why show up? What do I have to lose?" They just figured that they would come the following week. No big deal to them because if no money is being paid ahead there is no financial commitment on their part, only a verbal agreement or maybe a handshake. But it is a big deal to you because you are counting on the lesson fee money! I then decided to start collecting four weeks at a time. When I made this decision, I was so sure that everyone would quit. I was proven wrong with the exception of a few weak students. Most people liked the idea of paying ahead. So did I! The public that obtains music lessons for their children or themselves are usually in the middle or upper middle class and can afford it. Sure, some will struggle to pay, but just because they are not rich, it doesn't mean their money won't be there on the due date. Many in the lower income brackets are the best payers. At one time I taught five different doctors. Let me tell you, several think they are special because they don't carry a lot of cash on them. Of course, I am just using the doctor story as an example. This could be any high- income group for that matter. It sometimes seems that the ones with the most money want to hold onto it the tightest. You don't want them to quit because they are more than able to pay but they sometimes abuse their status and are delinquent. I just ask them right out for the money. The payer/student can come up with the lesson fee.

Delinquent Payments

Bad Checks

- This has never been an immense problem for me, but I do get a handful each year. This is a delicate circumstance and must be handled with kindness and respect. Try to give the check writer the benefit of the doubt because you do not want to lose their business. Why? Because they probably made an error. From my familiarity with these situations, most people are extremely embarrassed. I try to make it an 'easy to solve' problem. I have had *insufficient funds* stamped on checks from doctors, well-to-do people and those who live week to week. Most of the time the check writer will be informed of the bad check before you and bring in the cash. Since I bank online now, I have the advantage of almost immediate knowledge of when a student's bad check hits my bank account. My bank charges me $5.00 for this incident (your bank may differ, check and find out how they charge). The bank charge is added on to the student's check amount when the check payer is making good on the bad check. I have never had a problem getting the $5.00 because I tell them my bank charges me for this. I do not charge $20.00 for a bad check like some retail stores. That will be your call. I do not put a demeaning sign about bad check charges in my teaching studio or brochure. That would be just plain tacky. I just want to teach and play guitar. I can still make a living from that without trying to profit from other peoples misfortunes. I realize that the bad check scene does take up a lot of time and messes up the accounting books but it hasn't happened enough, from my business standpoint, to put up a bad check sign.

- **Another look at the bad check dilemma:** I just recently spoke with another teacher who has held a bad check from a student for over two weeks. The check amount is $15.00. The student has not returned to his lesson time spot since the bad check occurred. The teacher has been in phone contact with the person who is responsible for the check and they keep promising to come in and make it good. This has not happened. The teacher is charging $5.00 per missed lesson along with a $20.00 late fee and the amount of the bad check. So this student's bad check dollar amount is growing until the debt is paid.

These are two different scenarios. Make the decision that best works for you.

Late Payments

When the student is under 18 or someone else is responsible for their lesson fee, they sometimes keep coming in for their lessons, even when you haven't been paid. They will tell you they forgot or they will bring it in the following week or they left their checkbook at home and don't have enough cash on them. I tell them that I do not wish to wait a week for my money; they can bring it back later or mail it to me. Some people will push you to the limit when it comes to money. Don't let them. Take a stand. It's your money that they are playing with. These people almost always have the money! Many teachers charge a late fee for $5.00 a week. Again, call around (or check the Internet) to find out what is the average amount for a late fee for teaching in your area.

Partial Payments

Some payers will try to give you half of their due lesson fee, others will hand you a twenty dollar bill. Take it! Never turn down money. First of all, once you have the cash, it is yours. The bank won't accept promises at the drive-through window. Second, you do not want to insult anyone or appear to be ungrateful. Some payers could be having a rough week. If they are at least making an effort, work with them. Most people will come through with the rest of the due amount the following week. If they do not return, then you are the wiser for taking whatever cash they handed you. This hasn't been much of a problem for me because we do not charge that much money for our services. It's not like we are putting a transmission in someone's car and charging four figures. One student of mine comes to mind under this heading. He's a teenager who works and pays for his own guitar lessons without any outside help. He usually makes partial payments every two weeks. I have never had a problem collecting from him.

Receipts

Get a professional receipt book from an office supply store. The larger the receipt book, the better. This gives you more room to write any extra information needed on the receipt. Make sure that the receipt makes a copy for the student and one for your own records. Most receipt books have this capability.

- Every time that money exchanges hands, write a receipt and date it.
- If they give you a check, write the amount and check number on the receipt.
- Do the same for a money order.
- On the receipt, write down what lessons are being paid for, i.e. $100 for 3-11-04, 3-17-04, 3-24-04 and so on...
- Sign the receipt.
- Write the receipt and give it to them immediately upon receiving the fee.
- If they say, "I don't need a receipt", write it up and give it to them anyway. You will need it for your records. If they choose to forget it or throw it away it's their decision. You will have your record of that business transaction.

If you do not hand out a receipt it can come back to haunt you even in the best of situations. Remember this is just good common business practice.

I have used the back of my business cards for receipts when my receipt book wasn't available. Just put their name, date, amount paid for lessons, lesson dates, and sign it.

Small Business Philanthropy

You are a small business and helping those who cannot afford music lessons shows good social responsibility. I have given lessons away to the financially unfortunate student that can actually play an instrument and has an excess of potential talent. Sometimes up to six months worth. I do not spread the news of my philanthropy around because I do not want the whole world to start expecting complimentary music instruction, though the good word will travel. I personally do feel that I should give something back to the world because I remember when I was young, how different musicians at odd periods in my life helped me learn a new riff or two. Call it good karma, being nice or just doing what is right. For instance, I had two brothers, ages 8 and 9 performing an impressive classical guitar duet together in front of a crowd at a music store. How can I put a price on that?

However, I must admit, the free lesson theory has backfired on me a few times. For instance, a student not being grateful, not practicing, not showing up, just not caring...I nip that in the bud and sever those free lesson ties at once. But then again, if I feel the need to supply a needy student with free lessons, depending on the circumstances, I will certainly consider it.

Taxes

Find an accountant. Pay for their services and advice. Second hand information from a well-meaning family member or a friend isn't going to hold up.

Business License

Ask your accountant, check with your attorney and/or go to your county's business office.

What To Teach

Posture
It is imperative that the student practices good posture.

Sitting
- Do not let your student slouch. Insist that they sit up straight.
- If they must move their body to read off the music stand, make sure they move their chair. Do not let their leg hang over the chair's side.
- No feet dangling. Instruct the student to use the provided foot stool.
- Explain that the guitar's cutaway should go over the student's right thigh (unless this is a classical guitar lesson)

Standing
- If the student wants to lower their guitar strap so that the guitar is hanging by their knees, stop them! Explain how bad an effect this will have on their wrist. Tell them if they want to be cool, then learn to play correctly. Check out a photo of Jimi Hendrix. He wore his guitar fairly high up.
- Again, no slouching, have them stand up straight at all times.

'A' & The Lowdown on 'G'

Fill In The Blanks

Two 'G's Could Play the Bills

Reading Music ♫
I recommend teaching the skill of reading music to students that are still in school. I make this a requirement of my teaching agenda for ages 18 and younger. Parents are impressed with this and usually request it anyway. Students are use to the studying routine so they find the whole process fairly simple. Some adults ask about reading music for themselves but realize quickly that the process is time consuming for what they want to learn. Most adult students like to cut to the chase and start playing songs with familiar riffs and phrases right away. More on this in the **Ear Training** section.

- Reading music notes helps promote discipline. The student will have to focus to make this work. What better learning tool then focusing?
- The student's *picking* technique (see page 48) will develop with the correct fingering *and* put them on the road to playing the guitar in the proper manner. Bad habits will not have to broken in the future if the correct fingering technique is taught early on.
- I tell the student, numbered fingers #1, #2 and #3 will be played in the first three frets. This keeps the left hand in position with less movement. This is *my* teaching approach. It provides for less decision making when playing each indicated note. The new student does not have to choose which finger to use.
- Note positioning, combined with learning to read music will familiarize the new student with the location and tonal/pitch qualities of each note. Guitar students will use the treble clef.
- Teaching guitar students will also coincide with the teaching of bass guitar. The bass requires knowledge of the bass clef. Familiarize yourself with that area of music notation.

Vintage Music Instructional Book?

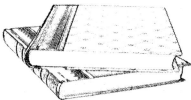

If the student has a guitar or music book that you do not use to teach with and you sense they want to use it, test it out, right then and there. There is probably something in it that you could use for that lesson. Keep an open mind. The book could be an old method from the 1950's with aged, yellowed pages that might have *the* missing guitar riff of all time! Fresh music should always be welcomed. These old books, sometimes as much as fifty years old, will have a dated look about them. Never laugh at their book. It could have belonged to a family member and might have some sentimental attachment.

Scales

According to *The Oxford Essential Dictionary* a music 'scale' is, quote: "arrangement of all notes in any system of music in ascending or descending order". Starting with a basic scale such as the 'C' scale, that uses no sharps or flats, will help the new student develop not only his picking technique but again help familiarize them with the location of each note. If they are teenagers and want to rock out, teach them a pentatonic scale. Let them have fun. What is the difference between the student learning "Twinkle, Twinkle Little Star" or a pentatonic scale? None really. They are new to the instrument, so why not teach them something that they will be able to use for the genre of music they like. The student needs to enjoy what they are learning. Though I would like to point out that the reason nursery rhymes are taught is because just about everyone is familiar with them and when an incorrect note is played in one of these pieces of music, it is known immediately. Allow the student to enjoy their education of the guitar. Keep them disciplined but not bored or insulted by childish songs.

While **picking** scales, teach the use of alternating picking. This will assist their guitar playing for the rest of their lives.

As far as a physical workout for hand muscles, I compare playing scales to working out in a gym, for your fingers. Beyond the musical education, scales build coordination. When the student develops musical thoughts and wants to explore those ideas they will flow more freely when played. Picking scales will liberate the imaginative musician and enable them to transform their inspiration into music. Music scales are a must! No one will be able to learn the correct way of playing or listening to music without the knowledge of scales. We, as teachers, owe that knowledge to the talented few that will stay with the instrument.

Some students will not enjoy playing scales. Show them how to have fun with them. Teach the A minor pentatonic scale, put a wah wah under their foot and have them jam along with a blues CD in the key of A minor. They will have the time of their lives! This will be an enriching and fulfilling experience for that student. They will feel they have achieved something musically. They have learned a new scale, improvised, used an effects pedal, and jammed with a great blues band.

Picking

Some students may have already created a set pattern to their picking skills before being taught by you. Work with the technique they have already developed. Make suggestions about various types of picking approaches (see below). Others, of course, are novices and are new to the whole guitar experience. You can teach what you think is the best picking technique for them. If you feel a student will become a serious musician eventually and has developed a bad-picking style, they will spend their entire musical lives trying to correct this mistake and it will affect their entire musical approach. Don't let this happen. Listed below are some variations of picking styles. Each style represents, in many cases, the genre of music that the student will be playing.

Variations of *Picking* styles:

- Flat – This is used in bluegrass. Tony Rice and Clarence White are prime examples.
- Alternating - The up and down picking, usually used in striking every note. Steve Morse, Zack Wilde, and Jimmy Bryant's fast picking approach.
- Downstrokes – Big in the blues area: B. B. King, Stevie Ray Vaughan and others have mastered this style.
- Classical/Flamenco – Andres' Segovia, Christopher Parkening and Paco DeLucia play these styles with their fingernails and thumb.
- Hybrid – The combinations of using a flatpick and your middle and ring fingers: Steve Howe and Albert Lee are excellent examples
- Thumb pick – Also known as the Travis picking style, Chet Atkins and Jerry Reed are the kings of this approach. The thumb pick and the use of your remaining fingers from the same hand, combined, creates full melodies with a self added bass line. But for that matter, Johnny Winter uses a thumbpick for the blues!
- Slappin'/Poppin' – Striking your thumb (from your picking hand) against the fretboard to create a percussive sound in unison with the note being played by your other hand.

These are just examples. Throughout guitar playing history, all kinds of picking techniques have been developed by crossing over into different music styles. This list is just an idea starting point.

The age-old question of how to hold a pick always comes up. Use your personal experience to explain this or do some research in various guitar instructionals for ideas on pick holding theory.

Keeping Rhythm

- Without rhythm there is no music. How can anyone take a solo if they can't play or feel the rhythm? Rhythm can be taught by using a metronome and/or a drum machine. These tools must be used in almost every lesson because the student needs to learn the importance of good timing and to keep you from having your chops and timing deteriorate because of playing with novices. My personal timing has gotten so strong that I can easily tell when a live drummer drags or speeds up, even if it is a minor occurrence. If you are a solo act this will definitely help. If you have a choice between using a metronome and a drum machine, go with the drum machine. They are a lot more fun and the students always find them fascinating. I usually let the student press the 'play' button on the drum machine and this keeps them involved with the exercise. Their involvement creates another positive vibe that keeps the spirit of learning better. To quote expert percussion instructor/author Mark Ellis, "It takes time to make time".
- This will help you improve dramatically as teacher/guitarist/musician and in such a short time *you* will be amazed.

Exercises

Picking scales is one exercise but you must coach the student to branch out and play a wide range of movements. In my book, *The Guy Lee Guitar Method©*, I have a variety of learning procedures that will give the student a wide array of guitar playing examples. Do your homework and be prepared for a variety of musical dialogue. Obtain an assortment of music teaching books and make annotations on what you might be able to use while you teach. I do this all of the time. I really enjoy it because it makes me a better guitar player and keeps me on top of things musically. Subscribe to as many guitar magazines as you can afford to. They always have great information and lessons. Don't shortchange yourself because you don't care for the band on the cover. Each one of these periodicals contains great columnists and guest writers that reveal some of their best guitar licks. Keep an open mind. Learn, learn, learn!

Here are some strum patterns that will make your student a more rounded guitarist:

- Chords – strum three different chords in 4/4 time. Try 'E', 'A minor' and 'D'. Have the student strum each chord four down strokes, one after another for ten minutes with a metronome or drum machine. This is one of the best exercises. Change out the chords and continue. You can always jam along. This will keep your lead chops in shape believe me. The student also enjoys the teacher's involvement. Time flies when you're having fun and when the student has fun they are usually absorbing all that they are learning. Now that's great teaching!
- Repeat the same process except replace the down strokes with *up and down* strokes.
- Just strum up strokes.

The idea is to be creative while teaching. The student will see this. They will benefit from these strumming patterns in many ways.

Showmanship
Showmanship is not exactly the ABCs of music education but it is definitely the XYZs. You should allot some lesson time to playing the guitar standing up with a strap on. This would only be for the more experienced and talented students. For instance, when playing a single lead note in the guitar's upper register on the first and second strings (beyond the 12th fret), a lot of your body's motion is used to push up those strings to reach the correct pitch. Let the student get familiar with what it takes to work through this ritual. Yes, I realize that you can sit down and bend strings too, but the physical input generated by the guitarist who must dig in to reach that *obtainable note* will generate an emotion that is somewhat different than the 'sit and bend' process. One way is no better than the other, but you owe it to the student to find out what works best for their style of music.

Self-Control
Itching, scratching, picking, whatever…needs to be contained. For instance, if a student is playing a pentatonic blues scale up and down the guitar's neck with a metronome clicking, do not let them stop to scratch their forehead, rub their arm or any other case of nervous action. The student needs to maintain self-control when playing an instrument. This is an important facet of learning a musical instrument. Let this be known early in their education so it will not be a problem later on.

CD/Chord Chart
The CD/Chord Chart (from books or periodicals) combination is an excellent way for your students to learn. You pick the exercise/song for the lesson. It doesn't mater if the student has heard the material before or not. Make sure that you use a music stand. Have a chord book ready because this will give the students another visual in addition to your hand on the guitar's neck. Learn four measures at one time if feasible. Teach the students the chords and have them play along with the accompanying CD track. Stop the track immediately when the four measures have been played. Only play the measures on the CD track that the students have learned. Take it one step at a time. Their timing and chord knowledge will increase dramatically.

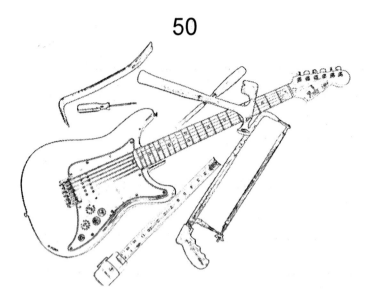

Guitar Care ♫

Yes, I repeat this a few times in this book but I like to approach it from different angles and situations. Here are a few tips:

- Teach the student to treat the instrument with respect. Do not let them bang it around, throw it in the case or bag or just plain abuse it in front of you. You must say something! You can explain calmly about taking care of the guitar. Tell them that they must value the instrument if they expect anything from it. Although it may appear as almost an inanimate object, like a piece of wood with metal wires to some, when in touch with the right pair of hands, some of the most beautiful music of all time will come from it.

- Keep it clean. Use a guitar cloth to keep the smudges off. Most of those cloths are chemically treated and work very well. This way, the ritual of polishing (with guitar polish only!) can be kept to a minimum. Some students will comment they can use a towel or a rag and they can, but they won't work as well as a guitar cloth. Encourage your students to spend a few buck$ and keep their guitar in good shape the correct way.

- How to set the guitar down. I'm sure you have been setting this instrument down for years but your students haven't been. Many guitarists (or any string instrument player for that matter) tend to lean the guitar on the back of the instrument's neck. They will set or lean it against a chair, an amp, a wall, a trashcan, or a table. Some people will lay it on the floor of your teaching studio. This will harm the instrument or at least put it in harm's way. Of course a guitar stand is the easiest and best way to protect your instrument from hitting the floor with a bang! But if a guitar stand is not readily available, tell the students to set the guitar on the string side of the fretboard. The neck won't get dinged. You can always replace a set a strings for a few dollars but a dinged-up guitar neck is something that the owner will have to live with. This is almost a daily occurrence while teaching.

- Keep those guitar strings* wiped off. Get the student in the habit of wiping the strings off after each lesson. The life of the strings will be extended. This is great advice to those whose money is tight or those who have palms that are sweaty.

Inform the student about the guitar's truss rod and how an adjustment will keep the string action down and the neck relatively straight. Many newfound guitarists do not realize that a neck adjustment can drastically improve any guitar.

Practice what you preach. Keep your guitar clean and dust-free. Let the students watch you take a guitar cleaning cloth and clean the smudges from your instrument as they play a scale or practice a rhythm.

*See page 35 for Changing Strings.

Ear Training

Back to the 'C' scale. Just singing the 'doe' 'ray' 'me'… alongside of the guitar notes is a great place to start. If the student doesn't have perfect pitch it does not matter. The student's musical ears can be trained to have good relative pitch and that is what you must attempt to do for the student. Of course some students can tap into the pitch source very easily and for others it might be a longer process. Be patient, you will make progress.

A handful of students throughout the years will say that they have perfect pitch or their parents will insist that they do. Most don't, but until you get to that point just nod and smile and stick to your method of teaching.

- **Teaching off of CDs** –Students bring in songs that they would like to learn off of a CD and I have them watch me pick out the chords, intro and/or the solo. This is one of the best and most inspiring ways to teach. The student's curiosity will be ignited and they will try to do the same.
- **Learning Riffs** – This builds up their Ear Training quickly. Teach them standard guitar riffs that they have heard their whole lives. Things like "Johnny B. Goode", "Day Tripper", "Smoke On The Water" or "Dueling Banjos". There are too many possibilities to list but you get the idea. Now there are a few students who haven't heard anything. So you will need to introduce them to some classic guitar riffs. Play the CD several times and let them absorb the music. Then teach it to them. Believe it or not, some students will look at their wristwatch impatiently, like you aren't teaching them anything; explain to them that this is an integral part of learning the guitar or any musical instrument. If you want to play music, you have to listen to music.
- **Singing Scales** – I do this for students all of the time. This is such a common practice it has become second nature to me. Singing the famous 'C' scale "Doe Ray Me Fa Sol La Tee Doe" and then playing it, gives the student a key ingredient of ear training. Just about everyone has heard this. Novices will relate to this musical phrase immediately. Sure, they will probably be too shy to sing around you, but they might try it in the privacy of their own home. What a great way to learn. But surprisingly to me, I have had a handful of people sing scales during their lesson.

Play some recordings of George Benson scat singing along with his guitar lines on "This Masquerade", or Johnny Winter matching note for note, voice to guitar, on his live version of "Mean Mistreater", to display the heights of the skill of knowing where the notes are located on the guitar.

♫♫♫♫♫♫♫♫♫♫♫♫♫♫♫♫♫♫♫♫♫♫♫♫♫♫♫♫♫♫♫♫♫♫♫♫♫

Many recordings are tuned a half step down to an 'Eb' instead of an 'E'. 99% of my teaching time, I will not tune down to 'Eb' for many reasons. I feel that my hearing is use to standard pitch. Even worse, the guitar, without its bridge being reset, never really gets in tune. The good side to staying in standard tuning (A=440HZ) is that the student will get to practice in flat and sharp keys. This will help them learn the root note names of all the chords. The all-so-common areas of the guitar will be played in new musical territories for a broader learning experience.

Self-Discipline

This isn't only good for learning to be a musician but will benefit you and your students for the rest of your lives. I can rightly state that any good musician has self-discipline. Sure, some people are born with talent and have inherited the ability and aptitude to play an instrument with ease. But that is only starters. If you want to be good, great or even superior at playing a musical instrument you must practice, practice, practice. This takes self-discipline and *many* hours each day if you want to become a respected professional in the music field. I am not talking about being famous. We all know that's luck, timing and being at the right place at the right time. I give kudos to the many famous musicians who are quite skilled and have had major success. Many others with lesser talent have achieved fame and success but little respect. Make sure that your student understands the importance of self-discipline. The other option is the Assignment Calendar (see **Assignment** on page 52) method in which the student is given specific daily practice routines.

Songs

It is important to select songs for your students to learn that fall into their age group and lifestyle. For the most part, you do not want to teach an 8-year-old child "Roundabout" by Yes. Or a teenager, who is ready to rock, "Michael, Row The Boat Ashore". Some students around the age of 60 enjoy playing "Buffalo Gals" and "When The Saints Go Marching In". Ask your students what songs they enjoy and move their future lessons in that direction. Even if the students can't play their instrument well enough yet to perform one of their preferred tunes, you can always simplify it and show them a key musical phrase. This will make students feel like they have accomplished a great feat and they have! About 80% of new students have heard a song that inspired them to pick up the guitar and that song was the seed that inspired them to start taking lessons. Find out which song it is and show it to them. The remaining 20% just have an interest in the instrument and will learn whatever you teach them. These 20% seem to have much patience and will learn and practice *your* way of instruction.

Teaching complete songs is a good habit to get into but sometimes a 30-minute lesson doesn't allow for it. Some students will let you teach them a riff from a song during their lesson. Their next lesson they are ready to move on. Others will stay on a piece of music until it is completed. For instance, "Stairway To Heaven" will take several 30-minute lessons before it is completed.

Learning A Song In Its Entirety
Pro – The students will have the self-satisfaction of completing a musical work.
Con – Be careful of your students getting burnt out on playing the same material over and over. If you sense the student is getting bored or restless, move on to some new material. Tell the student you can always come back to that song.

There will be many categories of songs to choose from because there is such a wide assortment of people who want to learn to play guitar. Below are some examples:

Children's Songs - Many songbooks contain elementary style songs such as "Mary Had A Little Lamb", "Twinkle, Twinkle Little Star", "Jingle Bells" and other child friendly song material. The reason for this is most of the world is familiar with these music pieces. When new students play these songs, most can recognize if they have played a bad note or not. I teach these styles of songs to the age group of 10 years old and younger. They work well and the kids have the satisfaction of playing these nursery rhyme musical themes successfully.

Partial Songs – On many occasions, students will just want to learn a signature riff, such as "Smoke On The Water", "Crazy Train" or "Johnny B. Goode". This is great way for them to build up their musical vocabulary with historic musical phrases.

Religious Songs – Many spiritual people will *only* allow their children to play songs from that genre. Today's religious music is well written, recorded and performed by some of the best musicians in the world. If they have CDs of the songs they like, start with that source of music. This is another reason to find out before you even sign the students up what kind of music they listen to. You don't want to start showing these new students some Ozzy or Iron Maiden and then realize that genre of music is not what they are paying to learn. Be thoughtful and ask before you start playing something that might make these new students uncomfortable.

Classical Songs – I teach at least two classical pieces to everyone. They love it and this material is great to put in their own personal songbooks. Beethoven's "Fur Elise" is very popular along with "Ode To Joy". Everyone has heard these songs from ages 7 to 70.

Rock Songs – Teenagers will ask you to teach them AC/DC's "Back In Black" because they have heard it a 1000 times and now they're ready to take that giant step and play it on their guitars. Adults are pretty much the same. They have their list of songs that they have grown up with and are ready to learn to play them. Many adults already play guitar and others will be new to the six string but they want to rock!

Reggae Songs – Hey Mon! Reggae is great fun to play and *everyone* loves playing it. Teach your students the A minor chord, set the drum machine to a reggae beat and have them strum on the up beat. They will be smiling and at the same time obtain a great feel for musical time. Everyone's a winner.

Country Songs – There's today's country music and yesterday's country music. You can usually make a judgment call from their age group.

Assignment Calendar

Assigning some students the task of a homework style music lesson is greeted with enthusiasm. Some people like the practice routine of seven minutes a day on scales, 15 minutes on barre chords and the other eight minutes on reading music notes. The habitual student has the need to be structured. Why? Because it is the way some people are. It takes all kinds to make the world go around and believe me; you will get students from all walks of life. When I first encountered the habitual students (which was almost immediately) I thought, "where's the passion, don't they want play music just for the love of it?" I found out quickly, no they do not. Not everyone wants to be a professional musician, some just want to be able to play their favorite songs, others want to lead youth groups with their guitars and for many it is just a hobby. Only a select few will ever take that giant step into the music business.

So making an assignment sheet of sorts will give the novice musician a routine practice schedule for them to happily follow. It will also clear any confusion about what to play during the seven days until their next music lesson. Basically it just keeps the learning of the instrument organized with a clear direction regarding practice.

This is a sample one week **Assignment Calendar** that I made on my computer. Notice that every day an assignment is written out for the student to follow. You can, for example, suggest a pre-determined minimum time limit to practice on each day or just write in what to practice and leave the time limit to the student's discretion.

June *Weekly Assignments*

Sun 6	Minor Pentatonic scale every fret-twice
Mon 7	Learn barre chords -first 12 frets 15 min
Tue 8	Minor Pentatonic scale every fret 25 min
Wed 9	Learn barre chords -first 12 frets 15min
Thu 10	Minor Pentatonic scale every fret-twice
Fri 11	Learn barre chords -first 12 frets 10 min
Sat 12	Barre chords & Minor Pentatonic scale 2004

After designing your own weekly **Assignment Calendar**, run off copies with a copier. It will be a more practical and inexpensive way of having many sheets to spare. If you have a file cabinet in your teaching studio, keep the copies in a folder.

A student, especially a new student, likes to take something tangible with them after their lesson. Not everyone is this way but many are. Some people feel that they have to have something material to show for the money spent on lessons.

Don't Be Sharp

A common problem among students when learning chords, regardless of their years or weeks of playing, is how much pressure they apply to the strings upon forming a chord on the guitar. The novice will press down way too hard on the strings, which will make a few of the notes go sharp and therefore make the guitar sound out of tune. This is a common occurrence. Point this out a few times and the student will remedy the problem themselves. This will help tremendously. Get them back in tune at once. Never let the tuning problem slide.

♪ Musicologist ♪

What me? Yes you. When teaching the guitar or any other instrument, having a background or information about your instrument is of the utmost importance. My experience from teaching is that students ask many questions about the source of the music that they are interested in. This relates to what I had mentioned earlier about obtaining books and magazines that help increase your familiarity regarding current musicians as well as information about those who have made an influential mark on music history. Educate the student on those musicians who may not be famous but have had an impact on the course of music. Use the teaching forum as an opportunity to introduce unsung music heroes. This could change the course of a young guitarist's musical journey. In return you will end up schooling yourself and growing as a teacher and a musician. This is a never-ending process. The students will have a great deal of respect for you and your knowledge. Respect goes a long way. This will help you retain your students and give you a reputation of being more then just some guitar player.

We Be Jammin'

Jamming has been one of the key elements of learning since the dawn of music. I encourage this almost spiritual music experience in my students by having them jam with other musicians and the teacher too. They will learn how to play rhythm, fills, new chords, solos, smooth out their timing and enjoy the fruits of their labor. Labor being of course, routinely practicing, attending their lessons, listening to music and reading subject matter that connects them to the guitar itself. The force of music comes through when two or more musicians perform together. The student's adrenaline will increase and help them discover their instrument on a different level. And as a perk, your playing abilities will ascend as well. It is just plain fun. This is an activity that I employ everyday.

Jamming doesn't have to be complex. Crank up the drum machine and just play two chords back and forth. Some of the best music made has been simple. A *jam* like this will present the student with a vehicle for improvisation and give them a chance to be creative. For instance, I will introduce four notes to the student to solo with and tell them to play only those four notes and the jam will never be out of tune. Sometimes they are hesitant if they are in the beginning stages of learning but I let them know that they will enjoy this approach to playing their guitar. The end result is that they will achieve a newfound confidence. What do you play? Just pick a music key and strum chords or grab a bass, i.e. if you are in the key of 'A', strum the chords 'A', 'G' and 'D' or if playing the bass, pick the single notes of the root. If the student is more advanced and if he/she is up to a higher musical challenge then go for it.

Make it standard practice to accompany students as much as possible during their lesson. This is a great way for them to speed up the stages of their improvement. Very rarely do I put my instrument down during a teaching session. I try to always be ready with a comment or a riff. The lesson will be all the more enjoyable if the teacher stays on the ball. Be a part of what the student is learning. Listen and contribute to that particular lesson's goal and help the student try to achieve it.

Professional Musicians?

Do any of your students desire to become full-time professional players? Do they understand that 99.9% (my own personal estimate) do not have complete financial success? Do they have what it takes to sacrifice for their craft? Are they willing to enjoy an almost Gypsy lifestyle with lots of travel and unknown adventures? Do they like to play their instrument every night? Pose these questions along with sharing some of your own personal experiences. Do not lean on the negative but try to give the students a balanced view of what they might expect. There is a **Professional Musician Quiz** on page 59 so that interested students can experience the level of dedication it takes to be a pro.

Solos

There are so many types and styles of guitar solos. Everybody wants to learn their favorite one. Solos are one of the many reasons people pick up the guitar in the first place. They have heard something that touches them musically and in return want to learn how to play it. Make the art of learning a complete solo an important part of your teaching agenda. Allow the student 4 to 6 lessons to learn a complete solo. Challenge yourself and your student. They like structure and learning complete solos will give them just that. With the audio clarity of CDs, the written availability of TAB and music notation music available, many solos can be transcribed or learned via sheet music/TAB.

Tone

Work with the student on getting a tone close to the original recording. This will help students understand even more how to dial in a certain sound with their gear.

Solos That Are Songs

Teachers would be wise to go back to the art of teaching complete solos. This way the students learn the value of structure. They will understand how a solo begins, what it will explore in the middle section and what kind of climatic ending will occur. The art of arranging a solo, if learned early, will be useful in building a strong foundation for serious musicians. Many songs are complete solos such as instrumentals. There are thousands upon thousands of great recorded instrumental/solos that can be transcribed by listening or by using sheet music/TAB. Many musicians just do this for the pure enjoyment of it. Here's a very short list as an example/starting point:

Albert Lee – "Country Boy"
Steve Howe _ "Clap" or "Mood For A Day"
Eddie Van Halen – "Eruption"
Eric Johnson – "Cliffs Of Dover"
Django Reinhart - "Minor Swing" or "Nuages"

Chet Atkins – "Yankee Doodle/Dixie"
Jerry Reed – "The Claw"
The Eagles – "Hotel California"
Maria Muldaur – "Midnight At The Oasis"
Duane Allman – "Little Martha"

Jazz musicians frequently pick out sax solos. Charlie "Bird" Parker's solos are probably the most popular.

Short Solos

George Harrison was the king of creative short solos. He put taste, tone and style into what have become classic songs. Have your students listen to songs by The Beatles. Their material is arguably the best examples of short solos. This group influenced many of the guitar solos of the 70's. Learn the melodic solo to "Something" or the rocking edge to "Let It Be" (from the original LP/CD) and the smooth lower register tone on "Michele". These solos are songs in themselves and can easily be sung or hummed on their own merit. Check out Bill Haley and The Comet's "Rock Around The Clock" for some sped-up tasteful guitar licks or the rhythmic solo from Buddy Holley's "Peggy Sue". Charlie Christian's "Seven Come Eleven" and "Solo Flight" great phrasing was inspired by the sax soloists of the 30's and 40's. A great solo is a great solo regardless of what year it was recorded. Learning a variety of solos from different eras will open many students' musical minds. While learning these solos, your students will have a hands on experience and music history lesson too.

Instructional Tips

1. **Enjoy what you are doing**

   ♪ I can't express the fun factor enough. I am not saying be a comedian but you do need to be in a great mood. If you had a tough day at home before coming in to teach, just remind yourself, "Hey, I have guitar in my hands, this is a good thing!" People can feel animosity and an uneven personality. Try to generate good vibes. I realize that this is an old hippie phrase but I'm sure you understand what it means.

2. **Make sure that the student is enjoying himself or herself**

   ♪ Let the student be part of the lesson. Don't be a know it all. Let them comment on the music they enjoy. Listen to them. Make the student a part of the learning process. If they are more involved it will make them feel like a part of the 'guitar-learning machine'.

3. **Be prepared for each lesson**

   ♪ Ask yourself, "Does the next lesson prefer bluegrass*? Hey, I'm a rocker man, I don't play bluegrass". Well if the student is paying you to learn bluegrass guitar licks then you better do your homework and teach that style to him or her. Believe it or not, it can be a lot of fun and challenging as well. Now I explain to the student that I want to teach them how to play the guitar in many styles so they will have to keep an open mind musically if they really want to grow as a player. Practice what you preach.

   This music genre example can be substituted for any other kind (rock, jazz, classical…).

4. **Punctuality is a must**

   ♪ Punctuality is like a pair of shoes*, everyone notices and it has a strong effect on your character profile. This sets an example for the *student* to never be late.

   Shoes: Oh yes, people will notice because you are always in a close proximity. Keep those dawgs clean.

5. **Don't show off, you are there to teach**

   ♪ Okay maybe we can't help it and for the most part it can contribute to the fun factor, but keep it short. It is good to remind the student what a dedicated guitarist you are. Just don't spend the entire lesson in your own guitarland with total disregard for their presence. Although I encourage you play some incredible guitar licks when people first meet you so they will want to learn from you.

6. **Utilize the lesson time**

   ♪ Utilize the student's lesson. Don't talk his lesson away. This is your responsibility. You can control your end of the conversation but sometimes they like to talk too. When the student reaches for air for the next sentence immediately ask the student to play a scale or chord. This will get them back into the rhythm of the lesson.

7. **Tie the loose ends of the lesson up**

   ♪ Allow the student time to put up their instrument. Some younger and elderly students need more time to pack up their gear. Don't keep your next student waiting or you will have to go over the designated time spot for that student. The snowballing effect on your next ten lessons is the risk.

8. **Eating**

   ♪ Do not eat around the students. Try not to be hungry during the lessons. Eat before you teach or when you take a break. Don't forget about using some type of breath freshener before the next lesson.

9. **Restroom Run**

   ♪ Just excuse yourself. No explanation needed. There is nothing to laugh about. Let's not embarrass yourself or your student.

10. **Teach, Play, Teach**

    ♪ Do not allow or encourage the student to talk their lesson time away. Many people love hear the sound of their own voice. Let them tell you whatever story that they want you to hear and as soon as they are finished quickly teach them a new chord or riff.

♫♪

57
♪ Musical Catch Phrases ♫

These may be common words to an experienced musician but this is a whole new language to new students.

Here is a list of musical terms and phrases that are used frequently during guitar lessons:

- ♪ a – *Anular (ring finger)*
- ♪ Action – *The height of the strings from the fretboard*
- ♪ Alternating picking – *Taking turns using the pick with up and down attacks*
- ♪ Arched – *The curve of a guitar's top*
- ♪ Arpeggio – *Picking a chord up and down*
- ♪ Bar line – *Separates the staff lines into measures*
- ♪ Basic Notes – *A, B, C, D, E, F, G*
- ♪ Bass Clef – *Used for low-pitched instruments*
- ♪ Bend – *Pushing or pulling the string to obtain a crying bluesy effect*
- ♪ Bending – *The art of pushing the string up or down*
- ♪ Bottleneck Guitar – *Slide guitar*
- ♪ Box – *Compact solo/lead area of the guitar neck*
- ♪ Break Song – *A loungey cornball tune played immediately before the band's break*
- ♪ Breakneck Speed – *Playing as fast as you can*
- ♪ Bridge – *The song's third section*
- ♪ Call and Response – *Playing off a vocal line or another musician's musical phrase; taking turns soloing back and forth*
- ♪ Cat – *A musician*
- ♪ Chops – *Your arsenal of licks and riffs*
- ♪ Chord – *A combination of notes played together*
- ♪ Chord diagram – *A block-like graphic of the guitar neck (frets & strings)*
- ♪ Chord Passage – *An arrangement of chords/notes that connects the song*
- ♪ Chord Progression – *A sequence of chords*
- ♪ Chord Shapes – *Different fingerings for the same chord*
- ♪ Chorus – *Usually the song's catchy part*
- ♪ Clone Tones – *Playing the same note on different strings*
- ♪ Cluster Voicings - *Two and/or three note combinations*
- ♪ Coda – *Tail, song's closing section*
- ♪ Comping – *Supporting another musician's playing musically*
- ♪ Connecting Notes – *Single notes that connect chords together*
- ♪ Count – *The song's time signature*
- ♪ Crank It Up – *Turn the volume up louder*
- ♪ Cross Picking – *Horizontally picking notes arpeggios across the guitar's neck*
- ♪ Crosspicking – *Skipping strings as you play*
- ♪ Crossing Strings – *The direction of each picking note when crossing to a different string*
- ♪ D.C. – *To the top. Go back and play from the beginning*
- ♪ D.C. al Fine – *Go back to the beginning and play until you reach fine Double Stop – Using two notes simultaneously for a riff*
- ♪ Downstrokes – *Picking the strings in a succession of down hits*
- ♪ Dropped 'D' – *Lowering the low 'E' string to a 'D' note*
- ♪ Dynamics – *Volume contrasts*
- ♪ Economical Fret Hand Fingering – *Using open strings during solos*

- ♪ Economy Picking – *Choice of picking strokes is determined by minimal movement*
- ♪ Enharmonic Notes – *Two notes that produce the same pitch*
- ♪ Feel – *Capturing the essence of the tune*
- ♪ Fine – *(fee' nay) Finish or end*
- ♪ Fingerboard – *The front side of the neck where the strings are played*
- ♪ Five Chords – *A5, D5, C5...Usually known as a power chord. Only the first and fifth note of the chord scales is played*
- ♪ Flat – *A note that is too low*
- ♪ Gig – *A performance*
- ♪ Groove – *The undercurrent vibe of the song*
- ♪ Guitar Octaves – *Nonadjacent string sets of the same note*
- ♪ Half step – *Move up or down one fret on the fretboard*
- ♪ Hammer On – *Strike the string once, get two notes going from low to high*
- ♪ Harmonic – *A bell like overtone*
- ♪ Harmonic Openess – *Using open strings (notes) along side of picked (fingered) strings*
- ♪ Harmony – *The relationship between two or more notes*
- ♪ Harp-like – *Combination of harmonics and open strings*
- ♪ Head – *Top of the song*
- ♪ Hexatonic Scale – *Six note scale*
- ♪ Humbucking Pickup – *Double coil guitar pickups that decrease hum, fat sounding tone popularized by Gibson©*
- ♪ Hybrid Scale – *Mixing each scales common tones resulting with a greater noted scale*
- ♪ i – *Indice (index finger)*
- ♪ Improvise – *Creating, in your mind, a melodic passage*
- ♪ Inside – *Playing solos safe within the natural scale*
- ♪ Interval – *The distance between two tones*
- ♪ Intro – *The beginning section of a song*
- ♪ Inversions – *Various chord forms with the notes in a different order*
- ♪ Jam – *Improvising with fellow musicians or a recording*
- ♪ Key – *Describes what notes work in the songs selection of chords*
- ♪ Key Signature – *The song's key can be recognized by the key signature with sharps and flats*
- ♪ Lay Back – *Play easy with lower volume*
- ♪ Lick – *A lead line that is used as a fill or solo*
- ♪ Lines/Spaces – *Sheet music location - E,G,B,D,F notes are located in the lines; F,A,C,E are in the spaces*
- ♪ m – *Medio (middle finger)*
- ♪ Measure – *Space between the bar lines on sheet music*
- ♪ Mode – *A succession of notes built from a scale degree other than notes*
- ♪ Modulate – *To change keys during the song*
- ♪ Monolithic Riffage – *Heavy rock chord/lead style*
- ♪ Music Staff – *Music notation is a written staff with 5 lines and 4 spaces*
- ♪ Muting – *Using you palm from your picking hand to lay lighting over the strings next to the guitar's bridge to keep the strings from ringing. This give a percussive effect*
- ♪ Notation – *Written music – notes or TAB style*
- ♪ Note – *A single musical defining pitch*
- ♪ Number System – *Nashville's simplistic, yet effective song chart method*
- ♪ Nut – *Holds the strings in place at the tuning key end of the guitar neck*
- ♪ Octaves Plus – *Using octaves while inserting 5ths & 4ths*
- ♪ Open Tuning – *Tune the six guitar strings to an open chord such as 'E', 'D', 'G' or 'A' or a self-developed tuning*
- ♪ Our-Of-Sync – *Lose timing while playing with a metronome or drummer*
- ♪ Outro – *The ending section of the song*
- ♪ Outside – *Playing solos more adventuress, using notes not usually within the natural scales*
- ♪ Overdrive – *Distortion*
- ♪ p – *Pulgar (thumb)*
- ♪ P-90 Pickup – *Gibson's© single coil pickup, darker sounding with definition*
- ♪ Palm Muted – *Keep strings from ringing freely with picking hand by guitar's bridge*
- ♪ Pedal Point or Tone – *Bass note*
- ♪ Pentatonic scale – *Five note scale*
- ♪ Pickup selector switch – *Chooses pickup combinations on multi-pickup guitars*
- ♪ Pickups – *The song begins with an incomplete measure, i.e. the first note is on the third beat*
- ♪ Pitch – *A degree of highness and lowness of a tone*
- ♪ Plectrum – *Guitar pick from England*

- ♪ Pot – *Poteniometer; used for the volume and tone controls*
- ♪ Pre-bent Notes – *Notes that are bent then picked*
- ♪ Pull Off – *Strike the string once, get two notes, going from high to low*
- ♪ R&B – *Rhythm and blues*
- ♪ Register – *The areas of voicings on the guitar's neck*
- ♪ Relative tuning – *Tuning the guitar by ear as close you can to standard pitch*
- ♪ Rhythmic Scratches – *Using the side of a pick aggressively while playing chords*
- ♪ Ride – *A solo or a lead break*
- ♪ Riff – *A musical phrase, usually the song's signature*
- ♪ Roll off – *Decreasing the output of the volume or tone knob*
- ♪ Rolling Arpeggio – *No not Mick's band. Picked with thumb and fingers or hybrid style*
- ♪ Rubato – *Free time*
- ♪ Saddle – *Part of the guitar's bridge, where the string lies*
- ♪ Scalloped Fretboard – *The neck's wood is scooped out to accommodate lower action and easier bending*
- ♪ Sharp – *A note that is too high*
- ♪ Shredding – *Fast distorted heavy rock stylings from the 1980s*
- ♪ Signature Lick – *An artist's recognizable sound of notes*
- ♪ Simple Time - *4/4, ℂ, ¾, 2/4 (time signatures)*
- ♪ Single Coil Pickup – *On coil pickup with a thin, twangy tone popularized by Fender©*
- ♪ Slash Chords – *Root being replaced in the bass, i.e. F/A or C/G*
- ♪ Slapping – *Popping your thumb against the guitar's fretboard for a percussive reaction*
- ♪ Slur – *A single note played at two (or more) different pitches*
- ♪ Solo – *Improvised or prearranged melodic notes, usually between the song's melody line or verses*
- ♪ Storytelling Solo – *The solo has continuity, usually from the vocal line with a beginning, middle and end*
- ♪ Strap button – *Holds the strap into place*
- ♪ Stretch – *Take a longer solo*
- ♪ String Drone – *Allowing a string (usually the low E or the E tuned downed to a D) to ring out while playing a melody*
- ♪ String gauge – *Thickness or diameter of a guitar string*
- ♪ Stringwinder – *A device for winding strings more rapidly*
- ♪ Stripped Down – *A song presented with very few instruments*
- ♪ Sweeping – *Fast notes results from efficiently approaching arpeggiated chords by raking the pick across the strings*
- ♪ TAB – *A newer musical notation system using numerals (representing frets) and lines (representing strings)*
- ♪ Tag – *A distinctive riff, usually heading towards the V chord*
- ♪ Tail – *End of song*
- ♪ Tapping – *Using the finger tips from your picking hand impacting the fretboard simultaneously while fretting with your other hand*
- ♪ Thumb Brush – *Pick or brush using the outside of your thumb*
- ♪ Timing – *Appropriate numbers of beats*
- ♪ Tone – *The sound of the instrument*
- ♪ Tonic – *Scale*
- ♪ Traditional Song – *Song in Public Domain; i.e. songs like Jingle Bells, Scarborough Fair, Greensleeves,*
- ♪ Transcribe – *Writing down the music/TAB/chords from a recording*
- ♪ Treble Clef – *Used for high-pitched instruments*
- ♪ Tremolo – *A device that produces volume fluctuations*
- ♪ Triad – *A three-note chord*
- ♪ Triple Stop – *Using three notes simultaneously for a riff*
- ♪ Tritone – *Three whole steps*
- ♪ Truss bar – *Located under the fretboard for neck adjustments*
- ♪ Tuning – *The process of how to keep your instrument in tune*
- ♪ Turnaround – *The chord or phrase that alerts the end of a chord sequence*
- ♪ Verse – *The song's main part*
- ♪ Vibrato – *Wiggling the strings*
- ♪ Voicing – *The sound of the same chord or selection of notes in various areas of your instrument*
- ♪ Walk – *Basslines up and down the guitar's fretboard*
- ♪ Whammy bar – *aka vibrato bar; loosens strings via the bridge resulting in shimmering chords or a dive bomb effect*
- ♪ Whole step – *Move up or down two frets on the fretboard except between E/F and B/C (only one fret)*
- ♪ Winging It – *Using your good pitch and knowledge to play an unknown song*
- ♪ Zigzagging Fingering – *Jumping and skipping strings and notes during a solo or riff*

Professional Musician Quiz

Are you one?   **Do you want to be one?**

1. If you had to choose between a CD player for your car or air conditioning, which would you select?

2. Would you rather go on a date this Friday night or play a gig at the local sports café?

3. Decide to buy the new, recently released hot guitar CD or buy yourself lunch?

4. On your *off* time, would you rather be watching reruns of the TV show Star Trek or jamming along with The Allman Brothers *Live At The Fillmore* CD?

5. Do you buy more than one set of guitar strings at one time?

6. Most of the time, do you wait until the last minute to set your rig up for a gig or do you get there early enough to take your time and test your gear?

7. Do you play your instrument everyday or about three or four days a week?

8. Will you accept money for your performances?

9. Do you like to travel?

10. Are you satisfied with the gear that you own and will probably never be interested in purchasing more instruments, effects or amps?

11. If you had an expensive instrument, would you pay ½ price plane fare for an additional seat to fly with your instrument in the seat beside you, if you could afford it?

12. Do you have cases and covers for you instruments and amplifiers?

13. Are you willing to smile and appear cheerful on every gig?

14. Do you own luggage?

15. Has a band rehearsal ever been canceled because someone you're dating wants to go the movies instead?

16. Have you ever purchased a vehicle with your music gear in mind?

Quiz Answers

1. CD Player
2. Play gig
3. Buy new CD
4. Jam with The Allman Brothers
5. Yes, buy multiple sets of strings
6. Try to arrive early
7. Play everyday
8. Making money makes you a professional
9. Yes
10. Never satisfied, always want more gear
11. If you can put it in your budget, then yes
12. Yes
13. Yes, all part of presenting yourself as a pro
14. If yes, then pack your bags and hit the road
15. If yes, get your priorities straight if you want to be a pro
16. It is the first thing you consider!

<u>Sample Flyer for "After Christmas Guitar Lessons"</u>
<u>Promotion</u>

Instruction by Guy Lee, guitarist and author of
The Guy Lee Guitar Method

Group Guitar Lessons

$100 Lesson Fee for eight one-hour group sessions
in **January & February**

THURSDAYS @ 8:00PM - AGES 12 TO ADULTS
SATURDAYS @ 3:00PM - AGES 6 TO 11

One week off after 4 lessons (01-29-04 [Thursday] and 01-31-04 [Saturday])

Lesson fee (**$100**) is due by
December 24.

The Guy Lee Guitar Method must
be purchased and will be used for
all lessons. The price is $19.95 +
TN sales tax of $1.95 = **$21.90**

Make all checks payable to:
Guy Lee

All lessons will be taught at
Mary's Music in Dickson, TN.

Gift Certificates available

TO CONTACT GUY LEE:
615-555-4668
PICKINGUY@AOL.COM
WWW.GUYTAR.COM

Sample Brochure for Group Lessons

A tri-fold, front print only brochure for group guitar lessons. Your PC or Mac can make a simple design like the one below and it will give the potential students information to take with them. A tear-off return application is included on 1/3 of the brochure. The prices are only an example. Check out the **Money** chapter (page 42) on how to evaluate what to charge. The **Group Lessons** (page 37) section of the book will give you more insight into brochure.

Group Guitar Lessons

Lessons will begin the first week of January 2004

**THURSDAYS @ 8:00PM
AGES 12 TO ADULTS**

**SATURDAYS @ 3:00PM
AGES 6 TO 11**

All group lessons will last one hour and will be taught at *Mary's Music* in Dickson, TN.

Instruction by **Guy Lee**- guitarist and author of *The Guy Lee Guitar Method*

Recommended for beginners

$XXX Lesson Fee for eight one-hour group sessions in January & February

One week off after 4 lessons (01-29-04 [Thursday] and 01-31-04 [Saturday])

Lesson fee (**$100**) is due no later then December 24.

The Guy Lee Guitar Method must be purchased and will be used for all lessons. The price is $19.95 + TN sales tax of $1.95 = **$21.90**

Learn to read music & TAB!

Make all checks payable to: **Guy Lee**

Gift Certificates available

**To contact Guy Lee:
615-351-4668
pickinguy@aol.com
www.guytar.com**

Contact Name:
Student's Name
Address:
City_____ZIP
State_____Phone
email:
Instrument_____Age

Use your imagination or the samples included in your software on your computer. If you teach in a music store, print 50 to a 100 brochures to start with and fold them carefully so they maintain a professional look. Put them on the store's front counter. Make sure that the stack doesn't run low.

<u>Sample Flyer</u>

Private

Guitar Lessons

At *Mary's Music* in Dickson
By **Guy Lee**

The lesson fee is $XX.XX on a monthly basis. The fee will be due at the first of each month. If a lesson is missed, it will be made up at the teacher's convenience. Call for details.

Every guitar student is required to purchase the instructional book,
The Guy Lee Guitar Method for lessons.
($19.95 + TN sales tax = $21.90)
Make all checks payable to Guy Lee

Guy Lee 615-555-4668
Mary's Music 615-555-4229

www.guytar.com

64

Blank sheet music for music notation will be helpful for the student's homework and the understanding of written music.

More Music Notes

Write in your own music notes. Best if using a pencil.

Keep on hand many blank pages of Tablature (TAB) for writing down riff and guitar lines for your students.

TAB Notes

Write in your own tablature. Best if using a pencil.

This blank sheet is used for the combination of TAB and music notation. This is the future of how music will be shown to new students.

Music Notation Staff Lines/TAB Lines

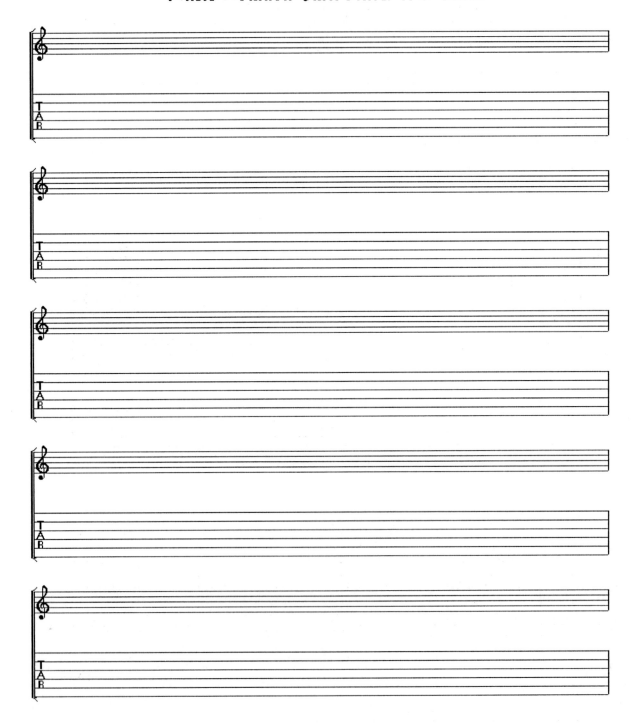

67

Writing out a chart on this blank page gives you options of using *Chord Blocks, TAB* and *Music Notation* in any combination.

100 Great Guitar Riffs

Introduce your students to some great playing and imaginative guitar exertion at its best!

Great riffs set the atmosphere for a song. Some are just simple chords. Others are intricate performances. Some, no matter what you're playing, if you have the right tone are going to sound great. No formula, just riffs. From the brain to the hand. In checking out this list I'm sure there's a few titles that you'll recognize instantly. But if you want to indulge a little and explore the other tunes that are unknown to you, you might hear a sound that will inspire that guitar of yours to jump into your hands immediately because you are so drawn to it. Maybe even start learning something new that you just have to have in your music vocabulary because it's so good. These songs range from number one Billboard charted songs to the obscure. They all seem to have that magical tone with the intensity that seems to move mountains, well at least makes you move your volume control clockwise. When hearing a life-changing riff for the first time, you go, "Wow!" and take a step back. It gives the mind a new seed to combat that stunted musical growth (that seems to happen to us members of the league of the frustrated guitarists) and revitalizes your outlook on music. I teach a lot of guitar students and I'm amazed at how many haven't heard what they need to hear (okay I'm preaching) so I thought this list would be a good starting point. When I began playing guitar in 1969, I went further back in time to learn the origination of certain tones. I tried to imagine what these cats were thinking, what influences were in the back of their minds. Studying songs and musician's styles stimulated my creative activity. So possibly these riffs might have a positive impact on you. I only allowed one riff per band, so this wouldn't be a Stones/Beatles article. Of course some of the same guitarists are in different bands. Commentary accompanies these riffs for a little insight. Here's the list of 100 Great Guitar Riffs because everyone loves a list.

1) *Can't You Hear Me Knockin'* – The Rolling Stones; Keith Richards opened 'G' tuning with his Les Paul through one of those early seventies Ampegs. After hearing this on the radio, it inspired me to list all these other riffs. A monster!

2) Anything by *Hendrix*, It's true, what can I say?

3) *Funk # 49* – The James Gang; Joe Walsh's Telecaster's burning intro that develops into a 'funky rhythm' all while being as one.

4) *Ticket To Ride* – The Beatles; Paul McCartney is a good guitarist himself and this one plays great on the second fret 'A' position.

5) *Drift Away* – Dobie Grey; studio giant Reggie Young's creativity played on a Les Paul makes this almost a song within a song.

6) *The Claw* – Jerry Reed; Reed's opening claw-picking on his gut string sets the tone for the whole song as well for this style of playing.

7) *Free Ride* – Edgar Winter Group; Dan Hartman, though not the guitarist in this band, wrote and played this intro on a great sounding Strat.

8) *Cold Turkey* – Plastic Ono Band; Sure it's not technical, but John Lennon's fury translates through those six strings on that capoed at the fifth fret Epiphone Casino.

9) *Statesboro Blues* – The Allman Brothers Band; Duane Allman had a touch and a special sound on his Gibson Les Paul (SG-style) through a Marshall. That young man passion and excitement was captured on this live rendition from The Fillmore.

10) *I Don't Need No Doctor* – Humble Pie; The performance of guitar team, Steve Marriott and Peter Frampton seized by this live recording with a three pickup Les Paul with humbuckers and TV model Les Paul with a P-90 in tow, made a powerful combination of tone for that 'E' 'G' 'A' power chord beginning to jump in your face!

11) *Walk This Way* – Aerosmith; Joe Perry and Brad Whitford rock hard on this one. American rock at its finest.

12) *Back In Black* – AC/DC; Malcolm Young's Gretsch with a Marshall, a signature rock sound unlike any other.

13) *That's Alright Mama* – Elvis; Scotty Moore's Gibson ES295 rhythmic drive pushed the King into the first rock and roll sphere.

14) *Won't Get Fooled Again* – The Who; Sure it's just an 'A' chord, but Pete Townshend's feel with the lethal combo of his orange Gretsch and Fifty's Fender Bassman makes it an 'A' to remember.

15) *El Paso* – Marty Robbins; Tone, timing and pure imagination starts this well-known country classic. Grady Martin's guitar testimonial.

16) *Le Freak* – Chic; This Strat influenced funk extravaganza created by guitarist/producer Nile Rodgers is one that is easy on the ears/hard on the fingers. What a vibe.

17) *Minor Swing* – Django Reinhardt; A signature piece for a one of a kind gypsy guitarist. Recorded in the Forties. Just amazing.

18) *Upsetter* – Grand Funk Railroad; A remarkable guitar tone on Mark Farner's Messenger guitar, with his stylistic rhythmic touch.

19) *Whole Lotta Love* – Led Zeppelin; Jimmy Page lays down his Tele and picks up a Les Paul and jumps on a Cry Baby wah wah for timeless monster On Led Zeppelin II.

20*) Listen To The Music* – Doobie Brothers; Tom Johnston cleverly plays E to A on the 9th fret on his Les Paul.

21) *Stray Cat Strut* – Stray Cats; Brian Setzer turned the heavy metal and pop world around with his big orange Gretsch guitar. You had to be there.

22) *Pride and Joy* – Stevie Ray Vaughn; Stevie's fat Start tone and that E string ringing alongside the E note on the B string on the fifth fret screams emotion.

23) *Beat It* – Michael Jackson; Eddie Van Halen plays the perfect solo for free.

24) *One Fine Morning* – Lighthouse; Amin, Bbmin, Bmin all played in a fast succession made this horn-inspired composition come alive.

25) *Roller Coaster (Of Love)* – Ohio Players; That chinking guitar part was always a ball to play. At the time during rehearsals all the non-guitarist would pick up my guitar on play that song.

26) *Papa's Got A Brand New Bag* – James Brown; Jimmy Nolen's rhythmic idea kicks off the Godfather of Soul's classic.

27) *I'm Goin' Home* – Ten Years After; Alvin Lee's famous 'Big Red' combined with his speed made my favorite Woodstock performance.

28) *Aqualung* – Jethro Tull; Martin Barre uses a straight rock tone from his Les Paul Junior.

29) *Iron Man* – Black Sabbath: Tony Iommi's tuned way down left handed SG help design many a young guitarist's first lick.

30) *Smoke On The Water* – Deep Purple; with Ritchie Blackmore's Strat, he never uses the middle pickup.

31) *Mrs. Robinson* – Simon and Garfunkel; grand acoustic guitar work

32) *Walk Don't Run* – The Ventures; A departure from Johnny Smith's original jazz piece. Mosrites a twangin'!

33) *Talks To Angels* –The Black Crowes: This open E tuning written by Rich Robinson is instantly recognizable.

34) *Stay With Me* – Faces; Ron Wood's years as a bass player for Jeff Beck must of given him some strong hands. Arguably his best work.

35) *Malaguena* - Intensive gut-string by whoever performed it.

36) *Hey Baby* – Ted Nugent; Byrdland + dedicated rock and roller = Hey Baby.

37) *Hold On Loosely* - .38 Special: Southern guitar rock pattern with lots of guitars and drums and vocals.

38) *Green River* – Creedence Clearwater Revival; most copied lick in the world next to Johnny B. Goode.

39) *Sweet Home Alabama* – Lynyrd Skynyrd; Ed King's Strat starts Skynyrd's most overplayed song. A total of three well placed electric guitars.

40) *Reelin' In The Years* – Steely Dan; Revolutionary in it's day, a Strat with a Humbucker in the rhythm position. Studio guitarist's Elliot Randall's Tour De Force.

41) *Johnny B. Goode* – Chuck Berry; The original rock and roll signature riff. Johnny Winter does a mean live version as well!

42) *Band On The Run* – Wings; McCartney and Denny Laine make tireless guitar notes. Great usage of electric, slide and acoustic 12 string guitars.

43) **Hey Bo Diddley** – Bo Diddley; Bo knows how to make his mark. Tremolo galore with an open chord.

44) **Woodstock** – Crosby, Stills, Nash & Young; It may sound easy, but to emulate this style is almost impossible. Lots of Gretsch White Falcons being played through vintage Fender amps.

45) **Barracuda** – Heart; Standard radio fare, but cool wang bar work.

46) **Detroit Rock City** - Kiss; Ace and his Les Paul, still holds up today.

47) **Life In The Fast Lane** – The Eagles; Joe Walsh's rockin' Strat begins, the others have to follow.

48) **Layla** – Derek and The Dominoes; Duane Allman's opening five note saga says it all.

49) **Messin' With The Kid** – Rory Gallagher; Rory's battered old Strat screams out one of rock's best hidden tracks.

50) **Sunshine Of Your Love** – Cream; Clapton's SG style Les Paul makes for a powerful arrangement.

51) **Led Boots** – Jeff Beck; Fusion with almost a demo like recording. Jeff and Jan Hammer compliment each well. He has a white Stratocastor on the LP cover.

52) **Black Magic Woman** – Santana; Like a voice. Carlos with a Les Paul and Fender Twin. This is before the Boogie and PRS days. How does he do it?

53) **Waitin' For The Bus** – ZZ Top; Garage bands all across the USA played incorrect versions of this. Bill Gibbons does it right though.

54) **Keep Your Lamps Trimmed and Burnin'** – Hot Tuna; Two versions, acoustic and electric, both are so musical, Jorma Kaukonen could probably pick one for you.

55) **Rebel Rouser** – Duane Eddy; The first musician to record in stereo. Fat tone from telephone line strings on his Gretsch with reverb from a water tank outside of the studio.

56) **Mississippi Queen** – Mountain; Gibson Les Paul Junior through a Sunn solid state amp head and Leslie West's vibrato.

57) **Rhiannon** – Fleetwood Mac; Lindsey Buckingham takes Stevie Nick's composition and puts a cool Amin riff in it.

58) **All You Love** – Magic Sam; Recorded in the 50's with not much technique but plenty of feel. A slightly distorted tremolo guitar sound.

59) **Still Got The Blues** – Gary Moore; A beautiful melody by Moore on his Heritage Les Paul.

60) **Cliffs of Dover** – Eric Johnson; Mr. Perfect's 335 fireball.

61) **American Woman** – The Guess Who/Lenny Kravitz; To tremolo or not to tremolo, Randy Bachman's three chord riff lives on and on and on…

62) **Carry On Wayward Son** – Kansas; Duel distorted guitars. Flawlessly in tune.

63) **Something To Talk About** – Bonnie Raitt; A slide melody that stays with you. Unforgettable.

64) **I Love Rock and Roll** – Joan Jett; Big chords. That E, A and B shovel down some real rock.

65) **My Girl** – The Temptations; One of Motown's clean, wonderfully picked hits.

66) **Running Down A Dream** – Tom Petty; Tasteful use of the low E string. Mike Campbell's ideas come across. I have only seen the man use single coil pickups.

67) **25 or 6 to 4** – Chicago; The late Terry Kath knew how to start this progression with his Gibson SG.

68) **Saturday Nights Alright For Fighting** – Elton John; The fuzzy guitar work of Davey Johnstone pushes hard through out the entire five minutes.

68) **Saturday Nights Alright For Fighting** – Elton John; The fuzzy guitar work of Davey Johnstone pushes hard through out the entire five minutes.

69) **Roundabout** – Yes: Steve Howe's classical guitar intro is timeless. On Yessongs he does the riff on electric.

70) **Last Train To Clarksville** – The Monkees; Louie Shelton played a Tele through a cranked Fender amp.

71) **Freedom** – Richie Havens; Powerful acoustic guitar work with an open tuning recorded live with mic at Woodstock.

72) **Give Me Love** – George Harrison; Harrison's clever slide: beautiful harmonies from his Strat.

73) **Don't Call Me Lonesome** –Radney Foster; Nashville studio guitarist Bill Hullet plays a Fender Nocastor through a very loud and hot (the tubes were about to explode!) Bassman for this country classic.

74) **Money For Nothin'** – Dire Straits; Knopfler with a Les Paul.

75) **Tell Mama** – Savoy Brown: Kim Simmons slide work is well done.

76) **Rock and Roll Fantasy** – Bad Co.; Phased, flanged, thick guitar sound from Mick Ralphs.

77) **Tobacco Road** – Rick Derringer; A mean 335 tone matching Edgar Winter's three octave voice. Tons of ideas flowing all at once.

78) **Boogie Chillin'** – John Lee Hooker: A guitar, a stompin' foot, and incredible feel.

79) **Soul Man** – Sam and Dave; Steve Cropper and his Tele makes this songs signature riff a classic.

80) **All My Rowdy Friends** – Hank Williams Jr; Double picked that fat E string over and over, but in time.

81) **Six Days On The Road** – Dave Dudley; Very cool. Recorded in the Fifties.

82) **Rumble** – Link Ray; Out of tune, distorted and very simple, but this is real retro.

83) **The Attitude Song** – Steve Vai; Very fast and melodic.

84) **The Pusher** – Steppenwolf; The art of rhythm guitar on probably the first anti-drug rock song.

85) **You Really Got Me** –The Kinks/Van Halen; The Kinks played it G to F, Eddie and the boys A to G.

86) **Solo Flight** – Charlie Christian; all down strokes, beautiful played. The tone that started it for jazz guitar.

87) **Walk Softly** – Kentucky Headhunters; Great use of an A chord and a Les Paul. This is country?

88) **Back To Square One** – Ernie Isley; Influenced by Hendrix, Eddie plays bad.

89) **Summer Breeze** – Seals and Crofts; Radio riff by Louie Shelton. Pure taste.

90) **Breezin'** – George Benson; When this came out everybody starting trying to play jazz and purchasing hollowbodies.

91) **Gimme Some Money** – Spinal Tap; I evol siht ffir! Derek Smalls says, " I hope you enjoyed that solo half as much as we did!"

92) **Country Boy** – Albert Lee; This is where all the chicken pickin' skyrocketed. Nashville owes this man, big time.

93) **Hideaway** – John Mayall; Clapton captured real magic on this cut. His use of open strings allowed the melody to flow.

94) **Show Me The Way** – Peter Frampton; Talk box combined with Django-type licks played with volume.

95) **Twin Guitar Special** – Bob Wills & His Texas Playboys; Steel and electric guitars played together are pretty scary. Recorded in 1941. Eldon Shamblin played the guitar and Leon McAuliff was on Steel.

96) **Mean Town Blues** – Johnny Winter; His guitar chops are remarkable. A lot of presence provided. Pure musical power.

97) **Honky Tonk Man** – Dwight Yoakum; Everyone that moved to Music City in the early Nineties new this Pete Anderson lick twice removed from the Johnny Horton song.

98) **Louie Louie** – The Kingsman; Anyone who started playing guitar in the Sixties learn this.

99) **Stratosphere Boogie**– Jimmy Bryant, the fastest guitarist to pick up a six string.

100) **Wildwood Flower** – Mother Maybelle Carter; fingerpicked acoustic guitar in the key of C. An original country classic.

Notes

Notes

Notes

About The Author

Guy Lee is a professional guitarist and accomplished writer. He recorded an album with the 1980's Southern California band Jawbone, who released the MTV video, "Did You See That Girl?". In 1989 he released a solo album, "Carolina" and toured Europe. During the 90s he recorded two CDs with the Bumper Cables and toured all over the Mid-West and Southeast. Guy is also a music journalist. His articles, reviews and interviews have been published in *Vintage Guitar, 20th Century Guitar, Bassics, Goldmine, American Songwriter, Home Recording* and several other periodicals. He was also the entertainment columnist for the Gannett paper, *The Dickson Herald*, for two years with his 'Guy Wire' weekly editorial.

Guytar Publishing has several more books that will be released next year. Check out the website at **www.guytar.com** for more information. Also on the website are lessons and performances by Guy Lee. Epiphone, RainSong, GHS Strings and Digitech endorse Guy.

♪♪

"I think you play just beautifully. You have a sweet touch and a unique approach that sings out clear."
Michael Allsup, guitarist - Three Dog Night

"Guy's not just a talented player, he's a great teacher".
Leo Lyons, bassist - Ten Years After

"Guy is one of the most versatile and talented guitarists I've had the pleasure to work with. The fact that he's also a gifted teacher and shares his knowledge in this book is even better"
Roy Vogt, bassist - Englebert Humperdinck, Jerry Reed, Dickey Betts

"Thanks to Guy anyone can learn how to play guitar easier than ever. I wish it were around when I started.
Maurice Johnson, guitarist - GIGORAMA software creator and author of 'Build and Manage Your Music Career'

"Guy's playing is thoughtful, evocative, good tone, pretty and has chops, hot licks. In a nutshell, if Pat Methany grew up on a farm".
Whit Smith, guitarist - Hot Club of Cowtown

"Makes clever use of haunting, floating augmented and diminished chords".
Don Barnes, guitarist -.38 Special

"Guy Lee is a player with killer chops and a teaching ability that is clear and concise - something that is hard to find in a guitarist. I'm sure you'll enjoy his method and learn much from it".
Shane Theriot, guitarist - The Neville Brothers

"Guy's playing hits all the nails right on the head...melody, chordal, rhythm...you name it, it's all there".
Ron Garant, publisher - Acoustic Fingerstyle Guitar & Bassics magazines

♪♪

The Guy Lee Guitar Method

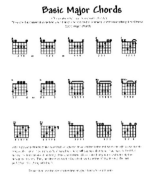

Basic Major Chords

ISBN 0-9747795-0-4

More Music Notes

'B' String Exercise

Music Notes & Other Assorted Lingo

Treble Clef

Bass Clef

Kinds of Notes

Cool Riffs in 'E'

The GuiStar Spangled Banner

Let's Learn Your ABCs

Learn and Teach:
Reading Music, TAB, Chords/Strumming & Ear Training
And much, much more!!!!!!! 80 pages with accompanying CD

Order *The Guy Lee Guitar Method* today for you and your students!

$19.95 with CD
Add $3.50 for shipping and handling
Tennessee residents add $1.90 per book for state sales tax

Send Check or Money Order to:

Guytar Publishing ©
6765 Forks River Road
Hurricane Mills, TN 37078

(931) 296-0938
(931) 296-9049 Fax

Or order directly from our Website
www.guytar.com

Make Checks payable to **Guytar Publishing**

Guy Lee has been teaching professionally for many years. His student body consists of more than 60 students a week: most of whom are taught on an individual basis. *The Guy Lee Guitar Method* is the result of perfecting his instructional skills. This book is for the beginner guitarist but fits in perfectly with intermediate players as well; even advance guitarists could learn a riff or two. *The Guy Lee Guitar Method* is split into two different basic approaches to learning the guitar, *Music Notation* and *Ear Training*. The *Music Notation* section is reading music notes and uses two fundamental time signatures, 4/4 and 3/4. Reading music develops the student's discipline and timing while putting into motion correct fingering and picking techniques. Tabulature accompanies each piece of music to prepare the student for the second section, *Ear Training*. This section has the student learning chords and strumming procedures that will give them a sense of rhythm. Also provided is a segment on some very cool guitar riffs. Guy's renowned "The GuiStar Spangled Banner" is written in tabulature with the accompanying chords. "Amazing Grace" is a simplified chord melody that can be performed as a solo piece at the beginner level. Other fun yet vital guitar riffs, scales, exercises and chords are provided for the student to branch out on. Only a minimum number of chords shapes are listed because from Lee's experience the students get overwhelmed from pages and pages crammed with chords. All of this will provide the student with a proven foundation that will give them good working habits and the correct approach to playing the guitar. An accompanying CD is provided.

Printed in the United States
25068LVS00001BA/7-56